Pass Your

Functional Skills Maths Level 2

Revise and Practice for your Functional Skills Maths Level 2 Exam

Alexander Christie

Functional Skills Maths
Level 2 Course

You
are
unique...

Virtual **exam mocks**

Personalised topic recommendations

Detailed **video explanations**

100's of practice questions

Learn on **your own schedule**

Expertly designed course

Shouldn't your **learning** be too?**

Get learning at pfs.la/courses

1

About this Guide

This guide has been written by a Functional Skills Maths expert, with the help of mathematicians, tutors and expert teachers, to create a comprehensive Functional Skills Maths Level 2 pocket guide that covers all aspects of the course, including the most up to date question types and solutions.

Using this guide is the best way to prepare for your Functional Skills Maths Level 2 Exam. It is relevant for all of the major exam boards, including AQA, Edexcel, City & Guilds, NCFE, Open Awards and Highfield Qualifications.

All of the content in the specification is covered within this guide, which is broken down into individual topics, targeted at splitting up your revision. Every topic is explained carefully, along with examples of how to answer different styles of questions you will see in the latest exam, including non-calculator methods. At the end of each topic there are QR codes that you can scan to see some more revision material and examples, along with worksheets and answers.

There are a few practice questions at the end of each section that will allow you to have a go yourself, along with answers at the back of the guide.

At the back of the guide you are gifted with exam tips aimed to help you pass your exam, along with all of the key formulas and rules you will need to remember for your exam.

3

Functional Skills Maths Level 2
Revision Fundamentals

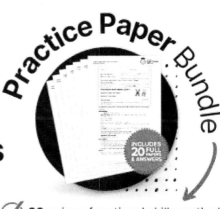

Practice Paper Bundle

INCLUDES **20** FULL PAPERS & ANSWERS

- ✓ **20** unique functional skills maths level 2 **practice papers** & **mark schemes**
- ✓ **Recommended** by **tutors** and **colleges**
- ✓ **Designed** by **experts**

Revision Cards

- ✓ **Recommended** by **students** and **tutors**
- ✓ Relevant to **all exam boards**
- ✓ Covers **all topics** in your exam

Revision Card and Practice Paper Bundle

- ✓ Papers from the **exam board** of your choice
- ✓ **Explanations, practice questions** and **exam questions** on every topic
- ✓ **Save** with the bundle **discount**

Fill your boots...
...with essential **revision supplies**!

Get prepared at pfs.la/shop

Contents

1 Numbers

1.1 Numbers and Place Value

Numbers are split up into columns, called digits. Each digit in a number has a different value depending on its position. The value of each digit decreases, going from left to right. The value for each digit added together makes the number. For example, 4721364 can be split up into these columns:

4	7	2	1	3	6	4
Millions	Hundred Thousands	Ten Thousands	Thousands	Hundreds	Tens	Units

To read, or write, a big number, you can break up the number into groups of three digits, starting from the right. For example,

4	721	364
Millions	Thousands	The rest

This number is read as: 4 million, 721 thousand, 364.

Or written as: four million, seven hundred and twenty-one thousand, three hundred and sixty-four.

Example 1

What is the value of the 3 in the number 23057?

3 is in the 4th column from the right, which is the thousands column.

So, the 3 is worth 3000 or three thousand.

Numbers can be positive, if they are more than 0, negative, if they are less than 0, or 0. Numbers lines can be helpful to visualise number problems. The further right you go, the bigger the number is:

For example, 3 is bigger than 1, which is bigger than −2.

Example 2

Which number is bigger, −14 or −8?

> As a trick, remember that since these two numbers are negative, the one which is bigger is the one with a smaller number after the minus (−) sign.
>
> So, −8 is bigger than −14.

For more revision, example questions and worksheets, scan this QR code:

1.2 Ordering Numbers

You can order numbers by putting them in order from smallest to largest or largest to smallest. Remember that a negative numbers with a bigger number after the minus (−) sign are smaller.

To order numbers, you will need to use follow this method:

1. Split the numbers into positive and negative.
2. Put the positive numbers into groups with the same number of digits and the negative numbers into groups with the same number of digits.
3. Put each group in order of size. Start by comparing the 1st digits, if these are the same then compare the 2nd digits and so on.
4. Write the numbers in their final order, remembering positive numbers are bigger than negative numbers.

Example 1

Put these numbers in order from smallest to largest:

$$172, 2134, 1391, 2290, 103$$

1. Split the numbers into positive and negative.	They are all positive
2. Put the numbers into groups with the same number of digits.	3 digits 4 digits 172, 103, 2134, 1391, 2290
3. Put each group in order from smallest to largest.	103, 172, 1391, 2134, 2290
4. Write the final order.	103, 172, 1391, 2134, 2290

Example 2

Put these numbers in order from largest to smallest

$$631, 62, -97, -95, 650$$

	Positive		Negative	
1.				
2. Split the numbers into positive and negative.	631,	62, 650,	−97,	−95
3. Put the positive numbers into groups with the same number of digits and do the same for the negative numbers.	3 Digits 631, 650,	2 Digits 62,	2 digits −97, −95	
4. Put each group in order from largest to smallest.	650, 631,	62,	−95, −97	
5. Write the final order.		650, 631, 62, −95, −97		

For more revision, example questions and worksheets, scan this QR code:

1.3 Addition and Subtraction

For addition, some questions may use the add symbol (+) or use the words "add", "and", "in total" and "altogether" and for subtraction, some questions may use the subtract symbol (−) or use the words "subtract", "minus" and "difference". These words will help you identify which calculation to use. However, sometimes in questions involving real-life situations you will not be told which calculation to use, and you will need to work this out. Some questions may even combine addition and subtraction.

Example 1

Students in a school in Year 7 must pick either Spanish, German or French. 72 students pick Spanish, 121 students pick German and 204 students pick French. How many students are there in Year 7?

Add together the three numbers. $72 + 121 + 204 = 397$

So, there are 397 students in Year 7.

Example 2

Millie has £155. She then receives £50 from her grandma. She then spends £78 on a new jumper. She owes her Mum £125 for rent. Does she have enough money to pay her rent?

1.	Add together £155 and £50.	£155 + £50 = £205
2.	Subtract £78.	£205 − £78 = £127

Millie has £127 left, so she does have enough money to pay her rent, since £127 is more than £125.

Addition and subtraction are opposite calculations, so you can use the opposite calculation to check your answer.

For some questions you will not be allowed to use a calculator, so you will need to know how to use the column methods for addition and subtraction.

Example 3 (Non-Calculator)

Yesterday, there were 1447 adults and 582 children that visited a tourist attraction. How many visitors were there yesterday in total?

1. Write the numbers one above the other, making the units line up. Draw a line beneath the numbers.

$$\begin{array}{r} 1447 \\ 582 \\ \hline \end{array} +$$

2. Add the numbers in each column and write the results beneath. If the result is 10 or more, carry the 1 to the left.

$$\begin{array}{r} ^{1\ 1}1447 \\ 582 \\ \hline 2029 \end{array} +$$

3. The final answer is the number on the bottom.

There were 2029 visitors

Example 4 (Non-Calculator)

Subtract 1827 from 3453

1. Write the numbers one above the other
    (with the bigger number on the top), making
    the units line up. Draw a line beneath the
    numbers.

    $$3453 \\ 1827$$ -

2. Subtract the numbers in each column and
    write the results beneath. If the number on
    the top is smaller, borrow a 1 from the digit
    to the left and reduce that digit by 1.

3. The final answer is the number on the
    bottom.

    1626

When subtracting using the column method, if you need to borrow 1 but the next digit
to the left is 0, then you must reduce this to 9 and borrow 1 from the next digit to the
left (and reduce the numbers you have borrowed from by 1) and so on.

For more revision, example questions and worksheets, scan this QR code:

1.4 Multiplication

Multiplication means so many lots of another number. For multiplication, some questions may use the multiply symbol (×) or use the words "multiply", "times", "lots of", "in total" and "altogether". These words will help you identify that the question involves a multiplication. However, sometimes in questions involving real-life situations it will not be obvious that you need to multiply. You will need to figure this out.

Example 1

Mr Johnson owns a shop. He buys 9 crates of cola. Each crate contains 24 bottles of cola, with each bottle costing £1.05. How much does Mr Johnson spend on cola altogether?

1. Find the cost of one crate by multiplying £1.05 by 24.

$£1.05 \times 24 = £25.20$

2. Multiply this by the number of crates, 9, to find how much Mr Johnson spends on cola altogether.

$£25.20 \times 9 = £226.80$

For some questions you will not be allowed to use a calculator, so you will need to know how to use the column method or grid method for multiplication. The grid method is easier to use, so this guide will focus on the grid method.

Example 2 (Non-Calculator)

Calculate 389×27

1. Draw a grid, writing the value of each digit in the calculation along the top and down the side.

×	300	80	9
20			
7			

2. Fill in each square of the grid, by multiplying each part of one number by each part of the other.

×	300	80	9
20	6000	1600	180
7	2100	560	63

3. Add up the answers from the grid (using the column method if you wish).

$6000 + 1600 + 180 = 7780$
$2100 + 560 + 63 = 2723$
$7780 + 2723 = 10503$

For more revision, example questions and worksheets, scan this QR code:

1.5 Division

Division is where you split up a number into smaller chunks that are equal in size. For division, some questions may use the divide symbol (÷) or use the words "divide", "division", and "split". These words will help you identify that the question involves a division. However, sometimes in questions involving real-life situations it will not be obvious that you need to divide. You will need to figure this out.

Example 1

Johannes needs to buy some fence panels. The fence panels come in packs of 5, and he needs 28. How many packs of fence panels does Johannes need?

Divide 28 by 5. $28 \div 5 = 5.6$

He cannot buy 5.6 packs, so he must buy either 5 packs or 6 packs.

5 packs wouldn't be enough, so he will need to buy 6 packs.

For some questions you will not be allowed to use a calculator, so you will need to know how to use the bus stop method for division.

Example 2 (Non-Calculator)

Calculate $292 \div 4$

1. Draw the bus stop. The number you are dividing goes inside, and the number you are dividing by goes outside.

$$4 \overline{\smash{\big)}\ 2\ 9\ 2}$$

2. Divide each digit in the bus stop one by one. Find how many times the number outside the bus stop goes into the number inside. Write this number on top and write the remainder to the left of the next digit inside. Repeat this for all digits.

$$4 \overline{\smash{\big)}\ 2\ {}^2 9\ {}^1 2} \quad 0\ 7\ 3$$

3. The number on top is the answer. 73

Example 3 (Non-Calculator)

Calculate $471 \div 5$

In the last step of this division the number does not divide fully.

So, you can either:

- Add a decimal point and extra 0's at the end of the number that is being divided.

$$
\begin{array}{r}
0\ 9\ 4\ .\ 2 \\
5\ \overline{|\ 4\ ^4 7\ ^2 1\ .\ ^1 0}
\end{array}
$$

- Say the answer with a remainder on the end.

$$
\begin{array}{r}
0\ 9\ 4\ r\ 1 \\
5\ \overline{|\ 4\ ^4 7\ ^2 1}
\end{array}
$$

So, the answer is either 94.2 or 94 remainder 1.

Multiplication and division are opposite calculations, so you can use the opposite calculation to check your answer.

For more revision, example questions and worksheets, scan this QR code:

1.6 Order of Operations (BIDMAS)

BIDMAS (or BODMAS) is an acronym used to remember the order in which to perform mathematical operations, going from left to right. The letters stand for:

- Brackets
- Indices (or Orders) – these are powers like squaring
- Division
- Multiplication
- Addition
- Subtraction

For division (D) and multiplication (M), work them out in the order they appear (from left to right) in the calculation. For addition (A) and subtraction (S), when they are the only two operations remaining, work them out in the order they appear (from left to right).

If you are using a calculator for BIDMAS, make sure you type the calculation in the correct order, and use brackets where necessary.

Example 1 (Non-Calculator)

Calculate $10 + (4^2 - 2 \times 2) \div 4$

1. Look inside the brackets first. In the brackets there is an index/power, a subtraction and a multiplication, so you need to do the index first, then the multiplication, and then the subtraction (since I is before M which is before S).

$$4^2 - 2 \times 2 = 16 - 2 \times 2$$
$$= 16 - 4$$
$$= 12$$

Now, the calculation is:
$$10 + 12 \div 4$$

2. Do the division next, since D is before A.

$$10 + 12 \div 4 = 10 + 3$$

3. Do the addition.

$$10 + 3 = 13$$

When a division is written as a fraction, work out the top and bottom using BIDMAS, and then see if you can simplify the fraction at the end.

Example 2 (Non-Calculator)

Calculate:
$$\frac{6 + 4 \times 5}{4 - (16 \div 8)}$$

1. Use BIDMAS on the top of the fraction.

$$6 + 4 \times 5 = 6 + 20$$
$$= 26$$

2. Use BIDMAS on the bottom of the fraction.

$$4 - (16 \div 8) = 4 - 2$$
$$= 2$$

3. Simplify the fraction if possible.

$$\frac{26}{2} = 13$$

For more revision, example questions and worksheets, scan this QR code:

1.7 Fractions

Fractions are split into the top and the bottom. The bottom is the number of total parts, and the top is the number of parts you are interested in. A division can be written as a fraction and vice versa.

Equivalent fractions are fractions that are equal in size but have different numbers on the top and bottom. For example, $\frac{1}{4}$ and $\frac{2}{8}$ are equivalent fractions:

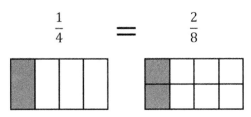

$$\frac{1}{4} = \frac{2}{8}$$

To go from $\frac{1}{4}$ to $\frac{2}{8}$ you multiply the top and the bottom by the same number, 2:

$$\frac{1}{4} \overset{\times 2}{\underset{\times 2}{=}} \frac{2}{8}$$

If the top and bottom numbers of a fraction are multiples of the same number, the fraction can be simplified to an equivalent fraction. A fraction is in its simplest form when the top and bottom numbers can no longer be divided to make whole numbers.

Example 1 (Non-Calculator)

Write the fraction $\frac{12}{42}$ in its simplest form.

1. Both 12 and 42 are divisible by 6, so divide the top and the bottom by 6.

    $$\frac{12}{42} \overset{\div 6}{\underset{\div 6}{=}} \frac{2}{7}$$

2. 2 and 7 are not multiples of the same number, so the fraction cannot be simplified any further. So, the fraction is in its simplest form.

    $$\frac{2}{7}$$

You can write one number as a fraction of another. You need to write the first number as the top of a fraction and the second number as the bottom. You then simplify the fraction fully if necessary.

Example 2 (Non-Calculator)

Write 20 as a fraction of 50 in its simplest form.

1. Write 20 on the top and 50 on the bottom.

    $$\frac{20}{50}$$

2. Simplify the fraction fully. Both 20 and 50 can be divided by 10.

    $$\frac{2}{5}$$

To calculate a fraction of an amount, you need to divide the amount by the bottom of the fraction and then multiply by the top number, or vice-versa.

Example 3

Find $\frac{3}{4}$ of £240.

1. Divide £240 by 4.   £240 ÷ 4 = £60

2. Multiply this by 3.   £60 × 3 = £180

Adding or subtracting fractions requires you to have two fractions with the same bottom number. If they aren't the same, then you need to turn them into equivalent fractions with the same bottom number. You then add or subtract the top numbers.

Example 4 (Non-Calculator)

Calculate $\frac{2}{3} + \frac{1}{4}$

1. Turn the fractions into equivalent fractions, so they have the same bottom number.

    $$\frac{2}{3} = \frac{2 \times 4}{3 \times 4} = \frac{8}{12}$$

    $$\frac{1}{4} = \frac{1 \times 3}{4 \times 3} = \frac{3}{12}$$

2. Add the tops of the fractions together.

    $$\frac{8}{12} + \frac{3}{12} = \frac{11}{12}$$

An improper fraction is a fraction where the top number is bigger than the bottom number. These are greater than 1. For example, $\frac{9}{2}$ is an improper fraction.

A mixed number is a mix of a whole number and a fraction. For example, $3\frac{1}{5}$ is a mixed number. You can convert between mixed numbers and improper fractions.

Example 5 (Non-Calculator)

Write $\frac{34}{5}$ as a mixed number.

1. A fraction is just a division. So, divide the top number by the bottom.

$$\frac{34}{5} = 34 \div 5 = 6\,r\,4$$

2. The whole number part of the division is the whole number part of the mixed number. The remainder goes on top with the dividing number on the bottom.

$$\frac{34}{5} = 6\frac{4}{5}$$

Example 6 (Non-Calculator)

Write $4\frac{2}{3}$ as an improper fraction.

1. Multiply the bottom number of the fraction by the whole number part of the mixed number.

$$4 \times 3 = 12$$

2. Add this to the top number of the fraction.

$$12 + 2 = 14$$

3. This number goes on top of the bottom number of the original fraction part.

$$4\frac{2}{3} = \frac{14}{3}$$

You can add and subtract mixed numbers using the skills you have previously learnt.

Example 7 (Non-Calculator)

Calculate $2\frac{1}{2} + 4\frac{3}{5}$

1. Split up the calculation into whole number parts and fraction parts.

$$2\frac{1}{2} + 4\frac{3}{5} = 2 + 4 + \frac{1}{2} + \frac{3}{5}$$

2. Add the whole number parts, and then the fraction parts.

$$2 + 4 = 6$$

$$\frac{1}{2} + \frac{3}{5} = \frac{5}{10} + \frac{6}{10} = \frac{11}{10} = 1\frac{1}{10}$$

3. Add the parts together.

$$6 + 1\frac{1}{10} = 7\frac{1}{10}$$

A subtraction is done using the same steps, except you need to subtract the parts instead of adding. However, you still add the parts back together at the end.

All types of fractions can be compared, whether it be normal fractions, improper fractions or mixed numbers. You can convert between these to determine which ones are bigger, and then put them in order if you need to.

Example 8 (Non-Calculator)

Which is bigger, $2\frac{2}{3}$ or $\frac{17}{6}$?

1. Convert $2\frac{2}{3}$ into an improper fraction, since improper fractions are easier to compare.

$$2\frac{2}{3} = \frac{8}{3}$$

2. The bottom numbers are different, so find equivalent fractions. Multiply the top and bottom of $\frac{8}{3}$ to get 6 on the bottom.

$$\frac{8 \times 2}{3 \times 2} = \frac{16}{6}$$

3. Compare the top numbers of the fractions.

17 is bigger than 16, so $\frac{17}{6}$ is bigger.

When using fractions on a calculator, if it doesn't have a fraction button then you can use the divide ($\div$) button instead. This will turn the fraction into a decimal, and then you can use these conversions in your calculations.

For more revision, example questions and worksheets, scan this QR code:

1.8 Decimals

Decimals are numbers with decimal points. They lie between whole numbers. For example, 0.2, 12.6 and 120.478 are all decimals.

The digits to the right of the decimal point also have values, just like for whole numbers. The value decreases the further right you move away from the decimal point. For example, 15.2387 can be split up into these columns:

1	5	.	2	3	8	7
Tens	Units		Tenths	Hundredths	Thousandths	Hundred Thousandths

You can add and subtract decimals using the same column methods used for whole numbers, you just have to line up the decimal points. Also, you may need to add 0's to the end of one of the numbers so that they have the same number of decimal places.

Example 1 (Non-Calculator)

Calculate $3.267 + 4.58$

1. Write the numbers one above the other, making the decimal points line up. Draw a line beneath the numbers. Add a 0 to 4.58 so that both numbers have three decimal places.

$$\begin{array}{r} 3.267 \\ 4.580 \end{array} +$$

2. Add the numbers in each column and write the results beneath. If the result is 10 or more, carry the 1 to the left.

$$\begin{array}{r} {\scriptstyle 1} \\ 3.267 \\ 4.580 \\ \hline 7.847 \end{array} +$$

3. The final answer is the number on the bottom.

7.847

Example 2 (Non-Calculator)

Calculate $11.28 - 6.75$

1. Write the numbers one above the other (with the bigger number on the top), making the decimal points line up. Draw a line beneath the numbers.

$$\begin{array}{r} 11.28 \\ 6.75 \end{array} -$$

2. Subtract the numbers in each column and write the results beneath. If the number on the top is smaller, borrow a 1 from the digit to the left.

$$\begin{array}{r} {\scriptstyle 0\ 10\ 1} \\ 11.28 \\ 6.75 \\ \hline 04.53 \end{array} -$$

3. The final answer is the number on the bottom.

4.53

You can multiply decimals in a similar way to how you multiply whole numbers, by using the column method or grid method. However, for decimals you need to follow these steps:

1. Convert the decimals to whole numbers, by moving the decimal point to the right.
2. Write down the number of decimal places that were moved in total.
3. Complete the column method or grid method to multiply without a calculator.
4. Move the same number of decimal places back at the end to get the answer.

Example 3 (Non-Calculator)

Calculate 3.89×2.7

1. Convert 3.89 and 2.7 to whole numbers.

    $$3.89 \rightarrow 389$$
    $$2.7 \rightarrow 27$$

2. Write the number of decimal places that were moved in total. There were two moved on 3.89 and one on 2.7

    3 places moved in total

3. Complete the multiplication. This was done in 1.4 Example 2.

    $389 \times 27 = 10503$

4. Move the same number of decimal places back, 3, to get the final answer.

    10.503

You can divide decimals in a similar way to how you divide whole numbers, by using the bus stop method. However, for decimals you need to follow these steps:

1. Write the division like a fraction.
2. Multiply the top and bottom by 10 repeatedly, until they are no longer decimals (i.e. they are whole numbers).
3. Complete the bus stop method to divide without a calculator. This gives the final answer.

Example 4 (Non-Calculator)

Calculate $2.92 \div 0.04$

1. Write the division like a fraction, with 2.92 on the top and 0.04 on the bottom.

    $$\frac{2.92}{0.04}$$

2. Multiply the top and bottom by 10 repeatedly to remove any decimals.

    $$\frac{2.92 \times 10}{0.04 \times 10} = \frac{29.2}{0.4}$$

    $$\frac{29.2 \times 10}{0.4 \times 10} = \frac{292}{4}$$

3. Complete the bus stop method to get the final answer. This was done in 1.5 Example 2.

    $292 \div 4 = 73$

Comparing decimals is like comparing whole numbers, but it can be a little harder.

Example 5

Put these decimals in order from smallest to largest:

$$3.76, 3.781, 3.01, 2.89$$

1. Add 0's to the end of and numbers so that they all have the same number of decimal places.

$$3.760, 3.781, 3.010, 2.890$$

2. Look at the numbers before the decimal point and order them from smallest to largest.

$$2.890, 3.760, 3.781, 3.010$$

3. Compare the 1st digit after the decimal point. Order them from smallest to largest. If they have the same 1st digit then compare the 2nd digits and order them. If they have the same 2nd digits then compare the 3rd and order them and so on. This will give you the final order.

$$2.890, 3.010, 3.760, 3.781$$

For more revision, example questions and worksheets, scan this QR code:

1.9 Rounding and Estimating

Rounding changes a number so that it is easier to perform calculations with. However, if you round too early in a calculation then it may make the final answer incorrect, unless you have been asked to round early in the question.

You may be asked to round to a number of decimal places, to the nearest whole number, or to the nearest 10, 100, 1000 etc.

Example 1

Round 16.127 to 2 decimal places.

1. Find the digit you are rounding to. Here, it is the 2nd digit after the decimal point.

$$16.1\underline{2}7$$

2. If the number to its right is less than 5 then you round down and it stays the same. If it is 5 or more then you round up and increase it by 1.

7 is bigger than 5

$$2 \rightarrow 3$$

3. Don't write any digits after this.

$$16.13$$

Example 2

Round 47.389 to the nearest whole number.

1. Find the digit you are rounding to. Here, it is the 1st digit before the decimal point (the digit in the units column).

    4<u>7</u>.389

2. If the number to its right is less than 5 then you round down and it stays the same. If it is 5 or more then you round up and increase it by 1.

    3 is smaller than 5

    7 → 7

3. Don't write any digits after this, or the decimal point.

    47

Example 3

Round 815 to the nearest 10.

1. Find the digit you are rounding to. Here, it is the digit in the tens column.

    8<u>1</u>5

2. If the number to its right is less than 5 then you round down and it stays the same. If it is 5 or more then you round up and increase it by 1.

    5 is 5 or more.

    1 → 2

3. Change all of the digits after this to 0's.

    820

Whenever you are rounding up, if the digit you are rounding is 9, then you have to round it up to 0 and add 1 to the digit to the left.

You can estimate answers to calculations by rounding the numbers in them to the nearest whole number, or nearest 10, 100, 1000 etc. This can be used to check your calculations are sensible or estimate the answer without a calculator. Normally, you will not be told how to round the numbers, you will have to use your common sense. However, you will usually be given leeway in your answers.

Example 4 (Non-Calculator)

Ishmael earns £9.86 per hour and works 8.25 hours in a day. He receives a bonus of £41.34. Estimate how much Ishmael earns on this day.

1. Round each number in the calculation to the nearest whole number.

$$£9.86 \rightarrow £10$$
$$8.25 \rightarrow 8$$
$$£41.34 \rightarrow £41$$

2. Perform the calculation.

$$£10 \times 8 + £41 = £121$$

You may have chosen to round £41.34 to £40. This would have been acceptable.

For more revision, example questions and worksheets, scan this QR code:

1.10 Percentages

Percent means 'out of 100' and is denoted by the % sign. For example, 30% means 30 percent, which is 30 out of 100. Percentages can be written as fractions and decimals. For example,

$$30\% = \frac{30}{100} = 0.3$$

You may be asked to find the percentage of something. To do this with a calculator, you will need to multiply it by the decimal equivalent of the percentage. To do this without a calculator, you will need to split the percentage up into smaller parts, such as 10%, 5% and 1%.

Example 1

There are 200 people at a party. 37% of the people there, are children. How many people at the party are children?

1. Find the decimal equivalent to 37%.

$$37\% = 37 \div 100 = 0.37$$

2. Multiply this decimal equivalent by 200.

$$200 \times 0.37 = 74$$

Example 2 (Non-Calculator)

Find 26% of 400.

1.	Split the percentage up into smaller parts.	$26\% = 10\% + 10\% + 5\% + 1\%$
2.	Work out the value of each part.	$10\% = 400 \div 10 = 40$ $5\% = 400 \div 20 = 20$ $1\% = 400 \div 100 = 4$
3.	Add up the parts.	$26\% = 40 + 40 + 20 + 4 = 104$

To express one number as a percentage as another number, you need to divide the first number by the second number, and then multiply the resulting decimal by 100, and add a % sign, to convert it to a percentage.

Example 3

What is 36 as a percentage of 120?

1.	Divide the first number by the second.	$36 \div 120 = 0.3$
2.	Multiply this decimal by 100 to get a percentage.	$0.3 \times 100 = 30\%$

You may be asked to calculate the percentage increase or decrease of something. For a percentage increase, you add the percentage increase to 100% and then convert this to a decimal to find the multiplier. You then multiply by this to find the increased amount. For a percentage decrease, you do the same but subtract the percentage decrease from 100% before converting to a decimal. The multiplier for a percentage increase will always be more than 1, and for a percentage decrease it will always be less than 1.

Example 4

Simeone has a salary of £25000. He is given a pay rise of 3%. What is his new salary after the pay rise?

1.	Add the percentage increase to 100%.	$100\% + 3\% = 103\%$
2.	Convert to a decimal to find the multiplier.	$103 \div 100 = 1.03$
3.	Multiply this by the original amount to find the increased value.	$£25000 \times 1.03 = £25750$

You could have worked out 3% of £25000 and added it to £25000 instead.

Example 5

Val owns a car. The price of the car last year was £7800. This year the value of the car has decreased by 5%. What is the value of the car this year?

1. Subtract the percentage decrease from 100%. $\qquad$ $100\% - 5\% = 95\%$

2. Convert to a decimal to find the multiplier. $\qquad$ $95 \div 100 = 0.95$

3. Multiply this by the original amount to find the decreased value. $\qquad$ $£7800 \times 0.95 = £7410$

You could have worked out 5% of £7800 and subtracted this from £7800 instead.

You may be given the original amount and the value after a percentage increase or decrease, and will need to find what the percentage change was using this formula:

$$\text{Percentage change} = \frac{\text{change}}{\text{original}} \times 100$$

If the answer is positive, then the change is an increase. If the answer is negative, then the change is a decrease.

Example 6

Calculate the percentage change of a concert attendance when it goes down from 1500 to 1200.

1. Calculate the change. $\qquad$ $1200 - 1500 = -300$

2. Put the values into the percentage change formula. $\qquad$ $\text{Percentage change} = \frac{-300}{1500} \times 100 = -20\%$

3. The value is negative, so it is a decrease. $\qquad$ 20% decrease

Sometimes you will be given the result of a percentage change and have to work backwards to find the original value. The method is the same whether the percentage change was an increase or a decrease.

Example 7

Hayley buys a cardigan in the sale. It is reduced by 20% down to £48. What was the original price of the cardigan?

1.	Calculate the cost of the cardigan as a percentage of its original value.	$100\% - 20\% = 80\%$
2.	Divide the cost by 80% to find 1% of the original value.	$80\% = £48$ $1\% = £0.60$
3.	Multiply by 100 to get the original value.	$100\% = £0.60 \times 100$ $= £60$

Alternatively, you could have converted 80% into a decimal, 0.8, and then divided £48 by 0.8 on your calculator to get £60.

For more revision, example questions and worksheets, scan this QR code:

1.11 Fractions, Decimals and Percentages

You can convert between fractions, decimals and percentages either when you are asked to, or when one of them suits a certain scenario. They all mean the same thing. Here are some common conversions that you will need to be familiar with:

Fraction	Decimal	Percentage
$\dfrac{1}{2}$	0.5	50%
$\dfrac{1}{4}$	0.25	25%
$\dfrac{3}{4}$	0.75	75%
$\dfrac{1}{5}$	0.2	20%
$\dfrac{1}{10}$	0.1	10%
$\dfrac{1}{20}$	0.05	5%

To convert:

- Fraction to decimal – treat the fraction like a division and divide the top number of the fraction by the bottom number of the fraction.
  For example,
  $$\frac{7}{20} = 7 \div 20 = 0.35$$

- Decimal to percentage – multiply the decimal by 100 (move the decimal point 2 places right) and add a % sign.
  For example,
  $$0.35 \times 100 = 35\%$$

- Fraction to percentage – just convert the fraction to a decimal and then the decimal to a percentage.
  For example,
  $$\frac{7}{20} = 0.35 = 35\%$$

To convert:

- Percentage to decimal – Divide the percentage by 100 (move the decimal point 2 places left) and remove the % sign.
  For example,
  $$35\% \div 100 = 0.35$$

- Decimal to fraction – write the decimal as a fraction with 1 on the bottom. Then, repeatedly multiply the top and the bottom of the fraction by 10 until the top number turns into a whole number. You can then simplify the fraction if necessary.
  For example,
  $$0.35 = \frac{0.35}{1} = \frac{3.5}{10} = \frac{35}{100} = \frac{7}{20}$$

- Percentage to fraction – write the percentage as a fraction with 100 on the bottom and then simplify if necessary.
  For example,
  $$35\% = \frac{35}{100} = \frac{7}{20}$$

You will need to be able to convert between fractions, decimals and percentages so that you can compare their size and order them.

Example 1

Put these in order from smallest to largest:

$$0.29, \frac{7}{25}, \frac{3}{10}, 27\%$$

1. Convert all numbers into the same form (decimals is usually easiest).

$$\frac{7}{25} = 7 \div 25 = 0.28$$

$$\frac{3}{10} = 3 \div 10 = 0.3$$

$$27\% = 27 \div 100 = 0.27$$

2. Rewrite the list as decimals.

$$0.29, 0.28, 0.3, 0.27$$

3. Put the decimals in order from smallest to largest, using the techniques you have already seen.

$$0.27, 0.28, 0.29, 0.3$$

4. Write down the order, changing the decimals back into their original form.

$$27\%, \frac{7}{25}, 0.29, \frac{3}{10}$$

For more revision, example questions and worksheets, scan this QR code:

1.12 Ratios

Ratios are used to compare how much of one thing there is to another. A ratio is written like 3: 4 and is spoken as "3 to 4". This ratio means that for every 3 lots of the first thing, there is 4 lots of the second thing. Ratios can be simplified, by dividing each part of the ratio by the same number each time, until they can no longer be divided.

Example 1

A structure is painted with 40 litres of red paint and 120 litres of blue paint. What is the ratio of red paint to blue paint, in its simplest form?

1. Write the relationship as a ratio.   40: 120

2. Simplify the ratio by dividing each number   40: 120
    by the same amount each time.   ÷ 10
                                                   4: 12
                                                                     ÷ 4
                                                   1: 3

This ratio cannot be simplified anymore, so the ratio is in its simplest form, 1: 3.

There are various types of ratio questions that you may encounter. You usually need to work out the value of one part of the ratio to be able to answer the question.

Example 2

Amy makes squash by adding 1 part squash to 6 parts water (1: 6). If Amy uses 30 ml of squash, how much water does she use?

1. You are told the value of 1 part of the   1 part = 30 ml
    ratio.

2. 6 parts of water are needed, so
    multiply the value of 1 part by 6.   6 parts = 6 × 30 = 180 ml

Example 3

Flatbread dough is made using 1 part flour to 2 parts Greek yoghurt (1: 2). 675 g of flatbread dough is made in total. How much flour is used?

1. Find how many parts of the ratio there are   1 + 2 = 3 parts
    in total, by adding up the parts in the ratio.

2. The flatbread dough contains 1 part flour.   675 ÷ 3 = 225 g
    Divide the amount of flatbread dough by
    the total number of parts to find how much   So, 225 g of flour is used.
    is in 1 part.

Example 4

Adam, Eve and Noah win a raffle prize of £600 and decide to split the money between them. The money is split in the ratio $4:1:3$ respectively. Work out how much money each of them receives.

1. Work out how many parts of the ratio there are in total.

$$4 + 1 + 3 = 8 \text{ parts}$$

2. Calculate how much 1 part is worth by dividing the prize money by the total number of parts.

$$1 \text{ part} = £600 \div 8 = £75$$

3. Find how much each person gets by multiplying the number of parts they have by £75.

Adam: $4 \times £75 = £300$
Eve: $1 \times £75 = £75$
Noah: $3 \times £75 = £225$

You can use ratios to calculate total amounts, using the following steps:

1. Work out the value of one part, or you may be given this in the question.
2. Work out the total number of parts.
3. Work out the total amount, by multiplying the value of one part by the total number of parts.

Example 5

A cookie mix is made using 2 parts maple syrup to 5 parts peanut butter. 60 g of maple syrup is used. How much cookie mix is made in total?

1. Find the value of 1 part, by dividing the amount of maple syrup by the number of parts of maple syrup.

$$1 \text{ part} = 60 \div 2 = 30 \text{ g}$$

2. Find the total number of parts.

$$2 + 5 = 7 \text{ parts}$$

3. Multiply the total number of parts by the value of 1 part to find the total amount of cookie mix made.

$$7 \times 30 = 210 \text{ g}$$

For more revision, example questions and worksheets, scan this QR code:

1.13 Proportion

If two quantities are proportional, then as one changes, the other changes in a specific way. You can use proportion to scale up or scale down amounts, such as in recipes.

Example 1

Janie has the following recipe for making ice cream:

500 g strawberries
200 g sugar
450 g crème fraiche

She wants to make a bigger batch of this ice cream. Calculate how much sugar she needs if she wants to use 800 g of strawberries.

1. Find by how much the amount of strawberries has increased, i.e. work out the scale factor.

Scale factor $= 800 \div 500 = 1.6$

2. Multiply the amount of sugar by the scale factor to find how much sugar she needs.

$200 \times 1.6 = 320$ g

This is an example of direct proportion. If two quantities are directly proportional, then as one increases, the other increases at the same rate. For example, as one is doubled, the other one is doubles, or as one is halved the other one is halved. You will see other types of questions involving direct proportion.

Example 2

Joe can run 8 km in 56 minutes. Assuming he runs at the same speed, how long would it take him to run 3 km?

1. Divide 56 by 8 to find how long it takes him to run 1 km.

$56 \div 8 = 7$ minutes

2. Multiply this by 3 to find how long it would take him to run 3 km.

$7 \times 3 = 21$ minutes

Inverse proportion is the opposite of direct proportion. If two quantities are inversely proportional, then as one increases the other decreases at the same rate. For example, as one doubles, the other one halves.

Example 3

It takes 3 people 120 minutes to paint a fence. Assuming they all work at the same rate, how long would it take 5 people to paint the same fence?

1. Multiply the number of people by the number of minutes, to find out how long it would take 1 person to paint the fence.

$3 \times 120 = 360$ minutes for 1 person

2. Divide by 5 to find how long it would take 5 people to paint the fence.

$360 \div 5 = 72$ minutes

When answering proportion questions, you need to assume that everything is done at the same rate. For example, workers working at the same rate or someone running at the same speed.

For more revision, example questions and worksheets, scan this QR code:

1.14 Formulas

A formula is a rule used to work out a value, and they may have one, or more than one step in them. You may see them written in words, where you will need to interpret the words and produce a formula from it.

Example 1

Simon gets a new mobile phone contract. The mobile phone company charge an initial £50 joining fee, and a monthly cost of £27. How much will Simon's mobile phone contract have cost him after 24 months?

1. Work out what calculations you need to do.

Step 1: £27 × number of months
Step 2: + £50

2. Put this into a single formula.

Contract cost
= (£27 × number of months) + £50

3. Put the missing numbers into the formula.

Contract cost = (£27 × 24) + £50
= £698

You may also need to convert words into letters or be able to use formulas given in terms of letters. For formulas using letters instead of words, you will need to replace each letter with a number. Some formulas don't use × and ÷, instead $a \times b$ may be written as ab and $a \div b$ may be written as $\frac{a}{b}$ for example.

For example, to work out the surface area of a sphere, you need to square the radius and multiply this by four lots of pi. In words, this is written as

$$\text{Surface area} = 4 \times \pi \times \text{radius}^2$$

or written using letters as

$$S = 4 \times \pi \times r^2 = 4\pi r^2$$

where S is the surface area and r is the radius.

Example 2

The cost of a hire car, in pounds £, is given by the formula $c = 0.8(30 + 10d)$ where c is the total cost and d is the number of days the car is hired for. Olly hires a car for 14 days. How much does this cost him?

1. Work out which letters you need to replace in the formula.

$$d = 14$$

2. Substitute this letter into the formula to find the total cost.

$$c = 0.8(30 + 10 \times 14)$$
$$= £136$$

For more revision, example questions and worksheets, scan this QR code:

Practice Questions – Numbers

Q1) Write the number 68373 in words.
[1 mark]

Q2) Put the following numbers in order from smallest to largest:

$$-278, 286, 301, 291, 38$$

[1 mark]

Q3) There were 5421 people at a concert on Saturday, and 8642 at a concert on Sunday. How many people were at the concert over the weekend?
(Non-Calculator)
[1 mark]

Q4) Calculate $2916 \div 9$
(Non-Calculator)
[1 mark]

Q5) Gladice uses 12 g of chocolate to make a biscuit. How many biscuits can she make using 558 g of chocolate?
[2 marks]

Q6) Calculate $6^2 \div (5 \times 2 - 7)$
(Non-Calculator)
[2 marks]

Q7) What is 40 as a fraction of 75? Write your answer in its simplest form.
[2 marks]

Q8) 38520 people vote for their local council in an election. $\frac{5}{12}$ of the people who voted chose to vote for the red party. How many people voted for the red party?
[2 marks]

Q9) What is $3\frac{3}{8} - 1\frac{1}{4}$? Write your answer as a mixed number.
(Non-Calculator)
[2 marks]

Q10) Find 5.86×23.1
(Non-Calculator)
[1 mark]

Q11) Mitch visits his local shop. He spends £4.80 on a gammon joint, £1.85 on some beans and £11.10 on some fizzy drinks. Estimate how much he spends in total.
(Non-Calculator)
[2 marks]

Q12) A venue has 800 seats. 38% of the seats have been taken. How many of the seats have been taken?
(Non-Calculator)
[2 marks]

Q13) A restaurant reduces the price of its signature dish by 12% from £15.50. What is the new price of the signature dish?
[2 marks]

Q14) The price of a rare pair of trainers increases in value by 16% to £145. What was the price of the pair of trainers before it increased in value?
[2 marks]

Q15) Put these numbers in order from largest to smallest:
$$0.79, \frac{3}{4}, 78\%, \frac{4}{5}$$
[2 marks]

Q16) 2500 ml of drink is split between three cups in the ratio $3:5:2$. How much drink will be in each cup?
[2 marks]

Q17) A mocktail is made from one part orange juice and four parts lemonade. 280 ml of lemonade is used. How much mocktail is made in total?
[2 marks]

Q18) Elise is making some buns. Her recipe tells her to use 200 g of flour for 16 buns. She only wants to make 12 buns. How much flour does she need?
[2 marks]

Q19) 3 people take 45 minutes to clean some cars. How long would it take 5 people to clean the cars?
[2 marks]

Q20) Sally wants to hire a bike. The bike hire company charges a fixed rate of £25 to hire the bike plus an additional £5 per day to hire the bike. Her friend Jessica hires a bike from a different bike hire company, that charges £8 per day. They both hire the bike for 7 days. Who spends the most money hiring the bike?
[3 marks]

Functional Skills Maths Level 2 Course

You
are
unique...

 Virtual **exam mocks**

 **Personalised** topic recommendations

 Detailed **video explanations**

 **100's** of practice questions

 Learn on **your own schedule**

Expertly **designed** course

Shouldn't your **learning** be too?

Get learning at pfs.la/courses

2 Measures, Shape and Space

2.1 Unit Conversions

All measurements need units, whether that's length, weight or capacity. The length of something is how long it is, the weight of something is how heavy it is and the capacity of something is how much it can hold.

You will encounter two main types of units, metric and imperial. You will also see other units. You will need to be able to convert between units to solve calculations.

Below is a table of common metric units and conversions you need to memorise.

Measure	Metric Units	Metric Unit Conversions
Length	millimetres (mm) centimetres (cm) metres (m) kilometres (km)	1 cm = 10 mm 1 m = 100 cm 1 km = 1000 m
Weight	grams (g) kilograms (kg)	1 kg = 1000 g
Capacity	millilitres (ml) litres (L)	1 L = 1000 ml

Below is a table of common imperial units and conversions. You will however be told these in the question, so you do not have to memorise them.

Measure	Imperial Units	Imperial Unit Conversions
Length	inches (in) feet (ft) yards (yd) miles (mi)	1 ft = 12 in 1 yd = 3 ft 1 mi = 1760 yd
Weight	ounces (oz) pounds (lb) stones (st)	1 lb = 16 oz 1 st = 14 lb
Capacity	fluid ounces (fl. oz) pints (pt) gallons (gal)	1 pt = 20 fl. oz 1 gal = 8 pt

The table below shows some other conversions you may see, but there are many more. Some of these are used to convert between metric and imperial units. Again, you do not have to memorise these.

Measure	Conversion
Length	1 ft = 30 cm 1 mile = 1.6 km
Weight	1 kg = 2.2 lb
Capacity	1 gal = 4.5 L 1 ml = 1 cm^3 1000 L = 1 m^3

The conversion factor is the number that multiply or divide by to change between two units. You can convert between any units as long as you are given, or know, the conversion factor.

For example, the conversion factor between centimetres and millimetres is 10. To convert from centimetres to millimetres, you multiply by 10, and to convert from millimetres to centimetres you divide by 10.

$$\times 10$$

$$1\ cm = 10\ mm$$

$$\div 10$$

Example 1

What is 3.4 kg in g?

1. Determine the conversion factor, using what you know.

$$1\ kg = 1000\ g$$
So, the conversion factor is 1000

2. To go from kilograms to grams you need to multiply, since a kilogram is bigger than a gram. So, you can work out your answer.

$$3.4 \times 1000 = 3400\ g$$

Example 2

Yuri puts 54 litres of fuel in his car. What is this in gallons?
1 gal = 4.5 L

1. Determine the conversion factor, using what you are given.

$$1\ gal = 4.5\ L$$
So, the conversion factor is 4.5

2. To go from litres to gallons you need to divide, since a litre is smaller than a gallon. So, you can work out your answer.

$$54 \div 4.5 = 12\ gal$$

Example 3

Pam has a bathtub with a capacity of 0.76 m^3. She fills the bathtub full with water. What volume of water does she put in the bathtub in litres?

$1000 \text{ L} = 1 \text{ m}^3$

1. Determine what the questions wants us to calculate.	The volume of water here is the same as the capacity of the bathtub, so you need to convert from m^3 to L.
2. Determine the conversion factor, using what you are given.	$1000 \text{ L} = 1 \text{ m}^3$ So, the conversion factor is 1000
3. To go from m^3 to litres you need to multiply, since 1 m^3 is bigger than 1 L. So, you can work out your answer.	$0.76 \times 1000 = 760 \text{ L}$

You may also need to convert between money currencies. These will always be given to you in the question.

Example 4

Julio arrives home from USA and exchanges 540 dollars ($) at an airport to pounds (£). The exchange rate is £1 = $1.35. How many pounds will he receive?

1. Determine the conversion factor, using what you are given.	£1 = 1.35 So, the conversion factor is 1.35
2. To go from dollars to pounds you need to divide, since a dollar is worth less than a pound. So, you can work out your answer.	$540 \div 1.35 = £400$

For more revision, example questions and worksheets, scan this QR code:

2.2 Conversion Graphs

A conversion graph is a straight-line graph that allows us to easily convert between units. One unit will be on the horizontal axis (x-axis) and the other will be on the vertical axis (y-axis).

Example 1

This conversion graph can be used to convert between pounds (lb) and kilograms (kg).

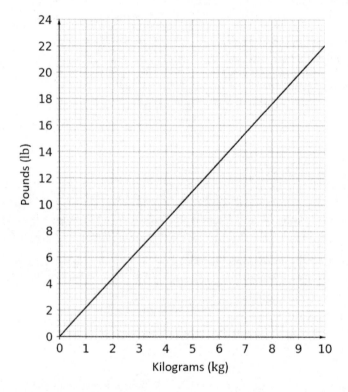

a) How many pounds is 5 kg?

1. Starting from 5 on the horizontal axis, move up until you meet the line.

2. From here, move across until you meet the vertical axis.

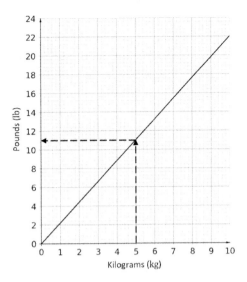

3. Read off the value to find the conversion.

$$5 \text{ kg} = 11 \text{ lb}$$

b) How many kilograms is 20 lb?

1. Starting from 20 on the vertical axis, move across until you meet the line.

2. From here, move down until you meet the horizontal axis.

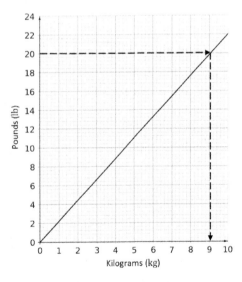

3. Read off the value to find the conversion.

20 lb is roughly 9 kg

For more revision, example questions and worksheets, scan this QR code:

2.3 Problems Involving Money

Most money questions you will encounter will have the units in pounds (£) or pence (p). You will need to be able to convert between the two as some questions may involve both.

- To go from pounds to pence, you multiply by 100

- To go from pence to pounds, you divide by 100

Example 1

Bruce buys a shoulder of lamb for £5.40, a pack of bacon for £1.80 and a sausage roll for 75p from his local butchers. How much does he spend in total?

1. Convert the price of the sausage roll from pence into pounds.

    $75p \div 100 = £0.75$

2. All prices are in pounds now, so add them up to find the total.

    $£5.40 + £1.80 + £0.75 = £7.95$

The rate of pay is the cost of something per unit time. For example, someone might earn £11.15 per hour or someone might pay £58 for their electricity bill per month.

Example 2

Jenna works one job as a pot washer and earns £9.70 per hour. She works 25 hours in one week doing this job. She also earns £60 one day in the week working at her local laundrette. How much does she earn in total this week?

1. Calculate how much she earns as a pot washer.

    $25 \times £9.70 = £242.50$

2. Calculate how much she earns in total.

    $£242.50 + £60 = £302.50$

Make sure you use the correct money format. Here, the answer is £302.50 not £302.5

You may be asked questions where you have to find the price of an something after it has been discounted or increased by a certain percentage. If something's price has been increased by a percentage, you add this value to 100% and then convert this value into a decimal to then multiply it by the original price. If a something's price has been reduced by a percentage, you take this value away from 100% and then convert this value into a decimal to then multiply it by the original price. This is very similar to percentage increase and decrease that you have seen in Percentages 1.10.

Example 3

James checks the value of his motorbike every year. Last year, the value of his motorbike was £12000. This year, the value of his motorbike has decreased by 10%. What is the value of his motorbike this year?

1. Subtract the percentage decrease from 100%.

    $$100\% - 10\% = 90\%$$

2. Convert to a decimal to find the multiplier.

    $$90 \div 100 = 0.90$$

3. Multiply this by the original amount to find the decreased value.

    $$£12000 \times 0.9 = £10800$$

You may also see discounts given as fractions.

Example 4

A suit costs £240. If there is a sale on which gives $\frac{2}{3}$ off the price, what is the new price of the suit?

1. Calculate $\frac{2}{3}$ of the original price.

    $$2 \div 3 \times £240 = £160$$

2. Subtract this from the original price of the suit.

    $$£240 - £160 = £80$$

Profit is the difference between the money you make from selling an item (selling price) and your costs. The percentage profit is the profit of selling an item as a percentage of the total costs involved.

$$\text{Profit} = \text{selling price} - \text{cost}$$

$$\text{Percentage profit} = \frac{\text{profit}}{\text{costs}} \times 100$$

Example 5

Tanisha buys a painting for £200 and sells it on for £250. Calculate her percentage profit.

1.	Calculate the profit.	$\text{profit} = £250 - £200$ $= £50$
2.	Calculate the percentage profit.	$\text{Percentage profit} = \dfrac{50}{200} \times 100 = 25\%$

For more revision, example questions and worksheets, scan this QR code:

2.4 Best Buys

Best buy questions require you to calculate different deals on products to work out which deal is the best value for money.

If you buy a pack of items, you can work out the price per item using:

$$\text{Price per item} = \text{total price} \div \text{number of items}$$

You can use the price per item to compare deals and find the best one. Sometimes you need to find the value of each deal for a common amount, such as finding the price of 100 g or 1 L (using Proportion 1.13). Some deals may also have offers on them too, which you will need to take into account.

Example 1

A shop sells chocolate bars in packs of 6 or packs of 15. The 6-pack costs £1.50, where as the 15-pack costs £3.30. Which pack is the best value for money?

1.	Calculate the price per item for the 6-pack.	$\text{Price per item} = £1.50 \div 6 = £0.25$
2.	Calculate the price per item for the 15-pack.	$\text{Price per item} = £3.30 \div 15 = £0.22$
3.	Make the conclusion.	The 15-pack is better value because it costs less per item.

Example 2

Bags of sand come in either 2 kg bags or 5 kg bags. The 2 kg bag costs £2.10. The 5 kg bag costs £5.40. Which bag of sand is the best value for money?

1.	Calculate the price per kg for the 2 kg bag.	$£2.10 \div 2 = £1.05$
2.	Calculate the price per kg for the 5 kg bag.	$£5.40 \div 5 = £1.08$
3.	Make the conclusion.	The 2 kg bag is better value because it costs less per kg.

You will not usually be told which common amount to use. Any suitable amount would work here such as 100 g or even 1 g, but finding the price per kg in this case was probably the easiest.

Example 3

Felicity wants to buy an airline ticket from either AirJetters or Cheap4Flights for her and her friend.

AirJetters	Cheap4Flights
£180 for 1 ticket 20% off on all tickets	£200 for 1 ticket get $\frac{1}{4}$ off on 2nd ticket

Felicity has a £50 off voucher for Cheap4Flights.

Which company should she use to get the best deal?

1.	Work out the total cost for AirJetters.	Price for 2 tickets = £180 + £180 = £360 Total cost after discount = $360 \times 0.8 = £288$
2.	Work out the total cost for Cheap4Flights.	1st ticket cost = £200 2nd ticket discount = $1 \div 4 \times £200 = £50$ 2nd ticket cost £200 − £50 = £150 Total cost = £200 + £150 = £350 Total cost after voucher = £350 − £50 = £300
3.	Make the conclusion.	AirJetters offers the best deal.

For more revision, example questions and worksheets, scan this QR code:

2.5 Interest and Compound Interest

Interest is a percentage of some money that is then added on to the total amount of money. For example, when you put money into a savings account it produces interest, or some loans require you to pay interest on top. This is similar to percentage increase in Percentages 1.10.

Example 1

Rory puts £8000 into a savings account that pays 2% interest per year. How much money does Rory have in his savings after 1 year?

1. Calculate 2% of £8000. $0.02 \times £8000 = £160$

2. Add this on to £8000. $£8000 + £160 = £8160$

Again, this could be done in one step: $1.02 \times £8000 = £8160$

Compound interest is where interest is added again and again. It is interest on money, which includes previous interest that has already been applied. For example, money saved in a bank account may earn interest every year ('per annum'), then the next year's interest will be calculated by taking into account the interest earned in the previous year.

Example 2

Giuseppe puts £2800 into a pension fund that earns 3% compound interest per annum. How much will the pension fund be worth after 3 years?

1. Find the total after 1 year. $1.03 \times £2800 = £2884$

2. Find the total after 2 years. $1.03 \times £2884 = £2970.52$

3. Find the total after 3 years. $1.03 \times £2970.52 = £3059.6356$

You will need to round this to the nearest penny (1p) since there are more than 2 decimal places. So, after 3 years the pension fund will be worth £3059.64

Some questions require you to work with money in other real-world contexts, such as evaluating a person's budget. A budget is a record of your money, used to show how much you can spend based on how much you earn. A budget may be shown in table or a list, with an amount of money associated to each thing.

Example 3

Simon is hosting a party. His budget is shown below.

Item	Amount (£)
Venue hire	£800
Food and drink	£250
DJ	£200

What percentage of his budget will be spent on the venue hire?

1. Find the total costs.

$$£800 + £250 + £200 = £1250$$

2. Find the cost of venue hire as a percentage of the total cost.

$$800 \div 1250 \times 100 = 64\%$$

Also, you may also be asked to calculate the amount of tax someone needs to pay or calculate someone's income after income tax. A tax is an amount of money that is paid to the government.

Example 4

Danny earns £32000 a year before tax. He isn't taxed on the first £12500 he earns (his "personal allowance"), and then pays 20% tax on all earnings above £12500. How much tax would Danny pay in one year, and how much would he earn after tax?

1. Work out his taxable income (the money earned over £12500).

$$£32000 - £12500 = £19500$$

2. Find 20% of this to find how much tax he would pay.

$$0.2 \times £19500 = £3900$$

3. Subtract this from his yearly earnings.

$$£32000 - £3900 = £28100$$

For more revision, example questions and worksheets, scan this QR code:

2.6 Speed

Speed is a measurement of the time it takes to travel a specific distance. Speed is usually measured in miles per hour (mph), kilometres per hour (km/h) or metres per second (m/s).

You can calculate speed, distance and time using these formulas and formula triangle:

$$\text{speed} = \text{distance} \div \text{time}$$

$$\text{distance} = \text{speed} \times \text{time}$$

$$\text{time} = \text{distance} \div \text{speed}$$

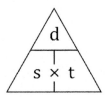

In this formula triangle, s represents speed, d represents distance and t represents time. The horizontal line means divide. For the one you want to work out, cover that letter and the remaining letters form the calculation you need to do.
For example, if you cover the d, then you are left with s × t.

You will usually be told what units to give your answer in for speed, distance and time questions. However, sometimes you may need to convert one or more of the units so they are suitable.

Example 1

Millie runs 2 km in 12 minutes. Calculate her speed in km/h.

1. Convert the time from minutes into hours, since you are asked to find the speed in kilometres per hour (km/h).

$$12 \text{ minutes} = \frac{12}{60} \text{ of an hour}$$
$$= 0.2 \text{ hours}$$

2. Calculate the speed using the correct formula.

$$\text{speed} = \text{distance} \div \text{time}$$
$$= 2 \div 0.2$$
$$= 10 \text{ km/h}$$

Example 2

A car moves at a speed of 12 m/s. How far does the car travel in 40 seconds?

Calculate the distance using the correct formula.

$$\text{distance} = \text{speed} \times \text{time}$$
$$= 12 \times 40$$
$$= 480 \text{ m}$$

Example 3

A cyclist moves at a speed of 10 mph. How long would it take the cyclist to travel 5 miles? Give your answer in minutes.

1. Calculate the distance using the correct formula.

   $\text{time} = \text{distance} \div \text{speed}$
   $= 5 \div 10$
   $= 0.5 \text{ hours}$

2. Convert the time from hours into minutes.

   $0.5 \times 60 = 30 \text{ minutes}$

For more revision, example questions and worksheets, scan this QR code:

2.7 Density

Density is a measurement relating the mass and volume of an object. You may see mass and weight interchanged, for this just think of them as the same thing. Density is usually measured in grams per cubic centimetre (g/cm^3) or kilograms per cubic metre (kg/m^3).

You can calculate density, mass and volume using these formulas and formula triangle:

$\text{density} = \text{mass} \div \text{volume}$

$\text{mass} = \text{density} \times \text{volume}$

$\text{volume} = \text{mass} \div \text{density}$

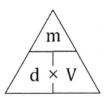

In this formula triangle, d represents density, m represents mass and V represents volume. This formula triangle works in the same way as the one in Speed 2.6.

You will usually be told what units to give your answer in for density, mass and volume questions. However, sometimes you may need to convert one or more of the units so they are suitable.

Example 1

Kim has a 400 ml of vinegar. She weighs the vinegar, and it weighs 420 g. What is the density of the vinegar in g/cm^3?

1. Convert 400 ml into cm^3 $400\ ml = 400\ cm^3$
   (remember $1\ ml = 1\ cm^3$)

2. Calculate the density using $\text{density} = \text{mass} \div \text{volume}$
   the correct formula. $= 420 \div 400$
                                        $= 1.05\ g/cm^3$

Example 2

An object has a density of 2.28 kg/m^3 and a volume of 0.8 m^3. Calculate its mass.

Calculate the mass using the $\text{mass} = \text{density} \times \text{volume}$
correct formula. $= 2.28 \times 0.8$
                                   $= 1.824\ kg$

Example 3

A block of iron has a density of 7.9 g/cm^3. What is the volume of the block of iron if its mass is 1.6 kg? Give your answer to 1 decimal place.

1. Convert the mass to grams. $1.6 \times 1000 = 1600\ g$

2. Calculate the volume using $\text{volume} = \text{mass} \div \text{density}$
   the correct formula. $= 1600 \div 7.9$
                                    $= 202.53 \ldots$
                                    $= 202.5\ cm^3$ (1 dp)

For more revision, example questions and worksheets, scan this QR code:

2.8 Perimeter

The perimeter of a shape is the total length of its outside edges. Sometimes you will not be given all of the lengths of the edges, so you will have to deduce or work out what the missing lengths are. The shapes you will be asked to find the perimeter of include squares, rectangles, triangles and composite shapes (shapes made up of smaller shapes).

Example 1

Below is a rectangle with a length of 12 cm and a width of 5 cm. Calculate the perimeter of the rectangle.

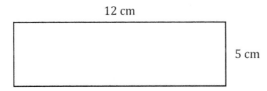

1. Find the missing lengths of the sides.

Opposite sides of a rectangle have the same length.
So, the missing lengths are 12 cm and 5 cm.

2. Calculate the perimeter by adding up all of the side lengths.

Perimeter = 12 + 12 + 5 + 5
= 34 cm

Example 2

Find the perimeter of the equilateral triangle below.

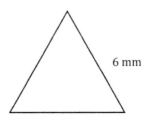

6 mm

1. Find the missing lengths of the sides.

All the sides of an equilateral triangle are the same length.
So, the missing lengths are both 6 mm.

2. Calculate the perimeter.

Perimeter = 6 + 6 + 6 = 18 mm

Example 3

Find the perimeter of the shape below.

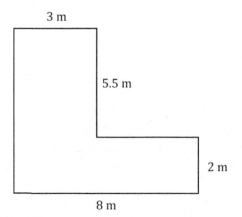

1. Find the missing lengths of all of the sides.

$2 + 5.5 = 7.5$ m
$8 - 3 = 5$ m

2. Calculate the perimeter.

Perimeter $= 8 + 7.5 + 3 + 5.5 + 5 + 2$
$= 31$ m

For more revision, example questions and worksheets, scan this QR code:

2.9 Area

The area of a 2D shape is the amount of surface it covers. Area is calculated by multiplying lengths together, so the common metric units for area are squared – mm^2, cm^2, m^2 etc. For imperial units for area, we usually say square inches (in^2) instead of inches squared, for example. Make sure all of the units are the same before you work out any areas.

There are some key formulas you need to learn to calculate the areas of squares, rectangles and triangles.

Area of square $= l \times l = l^2$

where l is the length of the sides.

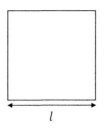

Area of a rectangle $= l \times w$

where l is the length and w is the width.

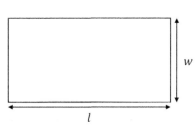

$$\text{Area of a triangle} = \frac{1}{2} \times b \times h$$
$$= b \times h \div 2$$

where b is the base and h is the height.

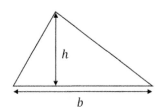

When calculating the area of a square or rectangle, the dimensions length, width and height might be interchanged.

Example 1

What is the area of this square?

3 cm

Multiply the length by itself.

$$\text{Area} = l \times l$$
$$= 3 \times 3$$
$$= 9 \text{ cm}^2$$

Example 2

John has a rectangular rug that has a width of 1.2 m and a length of 2.6 m. What is the area of his rug?

Multiply the width by the length.

$$\text{Area} = l \times w$$
$$= 1.2 \times 2.6$$
$$= 3.12 \text{ m}^2$$

Example 3

Calculate the area of this triangle.

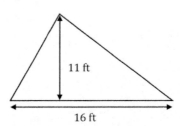

11 ft

16 ft

Multiply the base by the height and divide it by 2.

$$\text{Area} = b \times h \div 2$$
$$= 16 \times 11 \div 2$$
$$= 88 \text{ sq. ft}$$

You may be asked questions where you have to find the area of a compound shape. The easiest way to do this is to split up the shape into smaller shapes and find the area of those, and then add them together to find the total area. You may first have to find missing side lengths like on Perimeter 2.8.

Example 4

Find the area of this shape.

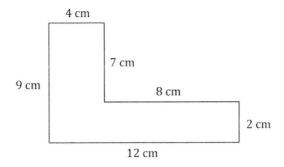

1. Split the shape into two rectangles.

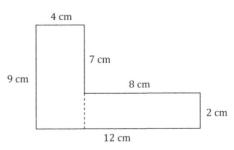

2. Calculate the area of the left rectangle.

Area $= 9 \times 4 = 36$ cm^2

3. Calculate the area of the right rectangle.

Area $= 8 \times 2 = 16$ cm^2

4. Add these together to find the total area of the shape.

Area $= 36 + 16 = 52$ cm^2

Notice that this shape looks like a large rectangle, with a smaller rectangle cut out of it. So, instead you could work out the area of the small rectangle and the large rectangle, and then subtract area of the small rectangle from the area of the large rectangle to find the area of the shape:

1. Work out the area of the large rectangle.

Area $= 9 \times 12 = 108$ cm^2

2. Work out the area of the small rectangle.

Area $= 7 \times 8 = 56$ cm^2

3. Subtract the small area from the large area to work out the area of the shape.

Area $= 180 - 56 = 52$ cm^2

For more revision, example questions and worksheets, scan this QR code:

2.10 Circles

You will need to be familiar with the names of parts of a circle:

- The circumference of a circle is the length around its outside – i.e. its perimeter.
- The centre of a circle is the point directly in the middle.
- The diameter of a circle is the distance from one side of the circle to the other, going through the centre.
- The radius of a circle is the distance from the centre to the circumference. The radius is always half of the diameter.

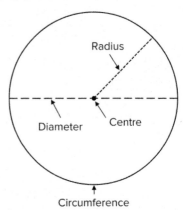

To calculate the area and circumference of a circle, you need to use a number called 'pi'. It is written with the symbol π. π is the ratio of a circle's circumference to its diameter (you do not need to remember this) and it is a decimal that never ends ($\pi = 3.1415926 \ldots$). If your calculator has a π button, then you can use this for calculations unless you are told to use 3.14 or 3.142 instead. They will all give slightly different answers, so use the appropriate one.

The formulas used to calculate the circumference of a circle are:

$$\text{Circumference} = \pi \times d$$

or

$$\text{Circumference} = 2 \times \pi \times r$$

where d is the diameter and r is the radius.
(Remember that the radius is half of the diameter).

The formula used to calculate the area of a circle is:

$$\text{Area} = \pi \times r^2$$

where r is the radius.

Example 1

Find the circumference of this circle.
Use $\pi = 3.14$

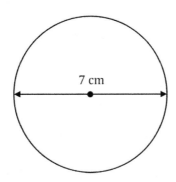

7 cm

Use the formula, and replace π
with 3.14

Circumference $= \pi \times d$
$= 3.14 \times 7$
$= 21.98$ cm

Example 2

Find the area of this circle.
Use $\pi = 3.14$

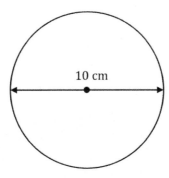

10 cm

1. Find the radius, since you are
   only given the diameter.

Radius $=$ diameter $\div 2$
$= 10 \div 2$
$= 5$ cm

2. Use the formula, and replace
   π with 3.14

Area $= \pi \times r^2$
$= 3.14 \times 5^2$
$= 3.14 \times 5 \times 5$
$= 78.5$ cm^2

Remember that the units for area are squared.

For more revision, example questions and worksheets, scan this QR code:

2.11 3D Shapes

2D shapes are flat objects, whereas 3D shapes are solid objects. The surfaces of 3D shapes are called faces.

2D shapes have 2 dimensions, for example length and width. 3D shapes have 3 dimensions, for example length, width and height (you may see these dimensions being interchanged, and also depth being used for 3D objects).

For example, the box below is 10 cm long, 7 cm wide and 3 cm high.

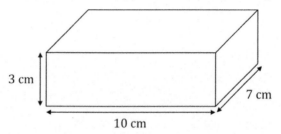

The dimensions of this box are 10 cm by 7 cm by 3 cm, which can be written as 10 cm × 7 cm × 3 cm.

You may get questions about 3D objects and their dimensions, so you need to know how to work with them.

Example 1

Henry is designing a container to hold 5 boxes of sweets. Each box of sweets is 20 cm long, 8 cm wide and 6 cm high. Sketch a container that could hold the boxes of sweets. Label the dimensions.

1. Work out how he could put them in a container.

He could put them side by side, like this:

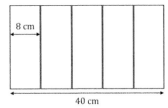

So, the container will need to be
8 × 5 = 40 cm wide.

2. Work out how long and high the container will be.

Each box is 20 cm long and 6 cm high, so the box will need to be at least 20 cm long and 6 cm high.

3. Sketch the container and label the dimensions.

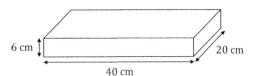

There will be a few different ways of answering this question.

You will need to be able to recognise and name these 3D shapes:

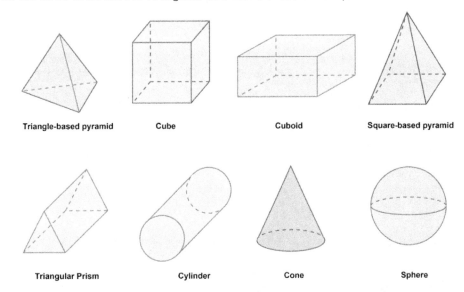

Triangle-based pyramid   Cube   Cuboid   Square-based pyramid

Triangular Prism   Cylinder   Cone   Sphere

60

- Cubes have square faces.
- Cuboids have square or rectangular faces.
- Pyramids contain a 2D shape as its base. The rest of the faces are triangles, which all meet at a point above the centre of its base.
- Cylinders, cones and spheres all have curved faces.
- A prism is a 3D shape in which 2 identical 2D shapes are joined together by rectangular faces. Therefore, cubes and cuboids are types of prisms.
- A cylinder is similar to a prism because its two end faces are identical – they are circles. However, they are not joined by rectangular faces, instead they are joined by a curved face.

For more revision, example questions and worksheets, scan this QR code:

2.12 Volume

The volume of a 3D object is the amount of space it takes up. Volume is calculated by multiplying 3 lengths together, so the units for length need to be multiplied 3 times too. So, the common metric units for volume are millimetres cubed (mm^3), centimetres cubed (cm^3) and metres cubed (m^3) etc. For imperial units for volume, we usually say cubic inches (in^3) instead of inches cubed, for example. Make sure all of the units are the same before you work out any volumes.

There are some key formulas you need to learn to calculate the volumes of cubes, cuboids, prisms and cylinders.

Volume of cube $= l \times l \times l = l^3$

where l is the length of the sides.

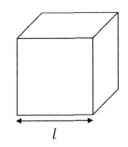

Volume of cuboid $= l \times w \times h$

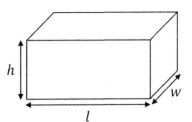

where l is the length, w is the width and h is the height.

Volume of prism $=$ cross-sectional area $\times$ length

where the cross-sectional area is the area of the front or back face.

Since a cylinder is like a prism, you can calculate the volume of a cylinder by:

Volume of cylinder $=$ area of circle $\times$ length
$$= \pi \times r^2 \times \text{length}$$

Where πr^2 is the area of one of its circular faces.

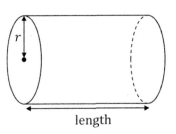

When calculating the volume of a cube or cuboid, the dimensions length, width and height might be interchanged. When calculating the volume of a prism or cylinder, height may be used instead of length.

Example 1

A cube has sides of length 6 cm. Calculate its volume.

Multiply the length by the length by the length.

$$\text{Volume} = l \times l \times l$$
$$= 6 \times 6 \times 6$$
$$= 216 \text{ cm}^3$$

Example 2

Calculate the volume of this cuboid.

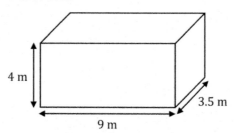

Multiply the length by the width by the height.

$$\text{Volume} = l \times w \times h$$
$$= 9 \times 3.5 \times 4$$
$$= 126 \text{ cm}^3$$

Example 3

Work out the volume of this triangular prism.

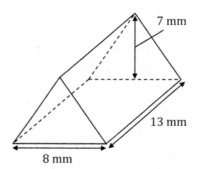

1. Calculate the area of one of the triangle faces.

$$\text{Area} = b \times h \div 2$$
$$= 8 \times 7 \div 2$$
$$= 28 \text{ mm}^2$$

2. Multiply this by the length.

$$\text{Volume} = \text{cross-sectional area} \times \text{length}$$
$$= 28 \times 13$$
$$= 364 \text{ mm}^3$$

Example 4

Calculate the volume of this cylinder.
Use $\pi = 3.14$

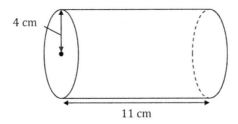

1. Calculate the area of one of the circular faces (remember to replace π with 3.14).

$$\text{Area} = \pi \times r^2$$
$$= 3.14 \times 4 \times 4$$
$$= 50.24 \text{ cm}^2$$

2. Multiply this by the length.

$$\text{Volume} = \text{area of circle} \times \text{length}$$
$$= 50.24 \times 11$$
$$= 552.64 \text{ cm}^3$$

For more revision, example questions and worksheets, scan this QR code:

2.13 Using Length, Area and Volume in Calculations

Some questions will require you to work out the length, perimeter, area or volume of an object as part as a larger calculation.

Example 1

Jamie is a runner. He aims to reach his target of running at least 8 km around the edge of the running track, made up of a rectangle and two semi-circles, seen below.

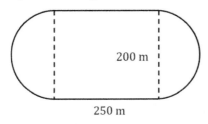

He can only complete full laps, i.e. he must finish the final lap even if he reaches his target of 8 km during the final lap. How many full laps of the track will he need to complete to do this?

Use $\pi = 3.14$

1. Work out the circumference of one semi-circle (this is half the circumference of a circle).

$$\text{Circumference} = \pi \times d \div 2$$
$$= 3.14 \times 200 \div 2$$
$$= 314 \text{ m}$$

2. Work out the perimeter of both semi-circles.

$$\text{Perimeter} = 314 + 314$$
$$= 628 \text{ m}$$

3. Work out the total perimeter of the running track.

$$\text{Total perimeter} = 250 + 250 + 628$$
$$= 1128 \text{ m}$$

4. Convert the distances so they are in the same units.

$$8 \text{ km} = 8000 \text{ m}$$

5. Find how many laps Jamie needs to run to reach his target.

$$8000 \div 1128 = 7.092 \ldots \text{ laps}$$

So 8 full laps

Example 2

Pauline takes part in an aerobics class at her local sports hall. The dimensions of the floor of the sports hall are shown in the diagram below. Each person needs 2 m² of floor space to meet health and safety standards.

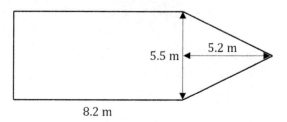

How many people can be in the aerobics class?

1. Find the area of the rectangular section.

$$\text{Area} = 8.2 \times 5.5$$
$$= 45.1 \text{ m}^2$$

2. Find the area of the triangular section.

$$\text{Area} = 5.5 \times 5.2 \div 2$$
$$= 14.3 \text{ m}^2$$

3. Find the total area of the floor.

$$\text{Total area} = 45.1 + 14.3$$
$$= 59.4 \text{ m}^2$$

4. Find the number of people that can be in the aerobics class.

$$59.4 \div 2 = 29.7$$

So 29 people

Example 3

Ben is filling a pool with water. His pool is 10 m long, 6 m wide and 2 m deep. He needs to add 1 L of chlorine to his pool for every 50000 L of pool water. Chlorine comes in 0.5 L bottles, costing £5.49. How much will Ben need to spend on chlorine for his pool? Use $1 \text{ m}^3 = 1000 \text{ L}$.

1. Work out the volume of the pool.

$$\text{Volume} = 10 \times 6 \times 2$$
$$= 120 \text{ m}^3$$

2. Convert the volume of the pool to litres.

$$120 \times 1000 = 120000 \text{ L}$$

3. Find the number of litres of chlorine that are needed.

$$120000 \div 50000 = 2.4 \text{ L}$$

4. Find the number of bottles of chlorine that are needed.

$$2.4 \div 0.5 = 4.8$$

So 5 bottles are needed

5. Find the amount it will cost Ben.

$$5 \times £5.49 = £27.45$$

For more revision, example questions and worksheets, scan this QR code:

2.14 Nets

A net is a 3D shape that has been unfolded. A net shows each face of the 3D shape laid out flat. 3D shapes usually have several different nets. For example, below are some examples of nets of cubes (there are many more):

Cube   Net of a cube

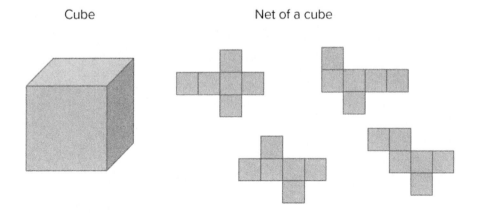

Each net can be folded up to make a cube, just like this one:

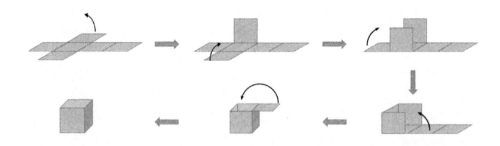

You will see nets of other 3D shapes too, such as cuboids, pyramids, prisms, and cylinders. Here are some examples of nets of these shapes:

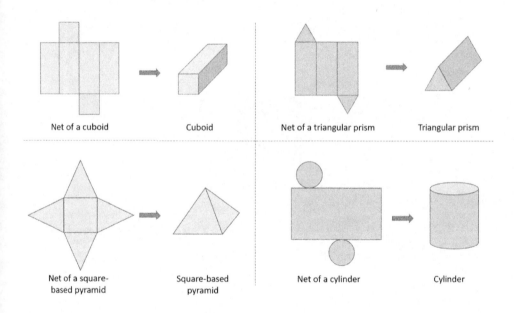

| Net of a cuboid | Cuboid | Net of a triangular prism | Triangular prism |

| Net of a square-based pyramid | Square-based pyramid | Net of a cylinder | Cylinder |

Notice that the net of curved side of the cylinder is actually a rectangle.

You will need to be able to draw nets of 3D shapes, using their dimensions. For these examples, there will be alternate ways of drawing them.

Example 1

Draw the net of this rectangle.

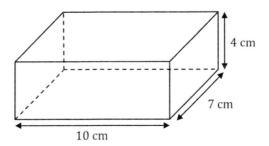

1. Draw the bottom face. Its dimensions are 10 cm by 7 cm.

2. Draw the side faces. The dimensions of these faces are 4 cm by 7 cm.

3. Draw the dimensions of the back and front faces. The dimensions of these faces are 10 cm by 4 cm.

4. Draw the top face. The dimensions of this face are the same as the bottom.

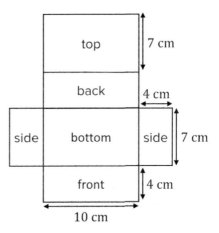

Example 2

Draw the net of this square-based pyramid.

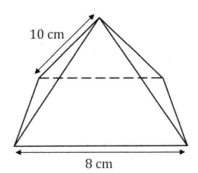

1. Draw the square base. Its dimensions are 8 cm by 8 cm.

2. Connect the base of each triangle to each side of the square base. The other two sides of each triangle are 10 cm, since they are isosceles.

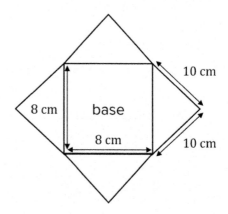

Example 3

Draw a net of this triangular prism.

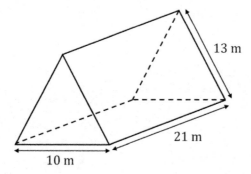

1. Draw the rectangles. Two of them are 13 m by 21 m and the other is 10 m by 21 m.

2. Connect the triangles, with the base of 10 m of each triangle connected to the edges of the rectangle with width 10 m.

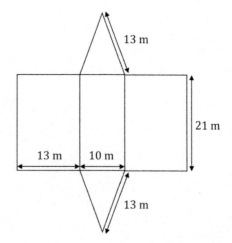

Example 4

Draw the net of this cylinder.
Use $\pi = 3.14$

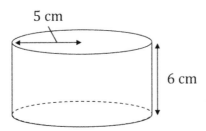

1. Find the circumference of the circles (the top and bottom faces). This is equal to the circumference of the curved face, which will be the equal to the width of the rectangle when it is flattened out.

    Diameter $= 5 \times 2 = 10$ cm

    Circumference $= \pi \times d$
    $\qquad = 3.14 \times 10$
    $\qquad = 31.4$ cm

2. The height of the rectangle is equal to the height of the cylinder. So, draw the rectangle.

3. Draw two circular faces connected to the rectangle along its circumference, with one on each side.

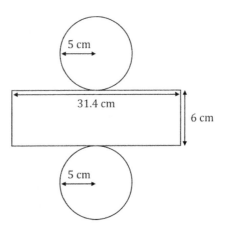

For more revision, example questions and worksheets, scan this QR code:

2.15 Surface Area

The surface area of a 3D shape is the area of all of the faces of the shape added together. You could be given the area of each face of a 3D shape, or you will more likely be given the dimensions of the 3D shape and have to work out the area of each face individually.

Example 1

Calculate the surface area of a cube with sides of length 3 cm.

1. A cube has 6 identical square faces. So, calculate the area of one face.

$$\text{Area of face} = 3 \times 3$$
$$= 9 \text{ cm}^2$$

2. The surface area is 6 lots of this face (or the area of each face added together).

$$\text{Surface area} = 6 \times 9$$
$$= 54 \text{ cm}^2$$

Example 2

Calculate the surface area of this cuboid.

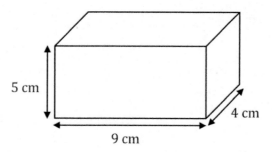

1. Calculate the area of the front or back face.

$$\text{Area of face} = 9 \times 5$$
$$= 45 \text{ cm}^2$$

2. Calculate the area of the top or bottom face.

$$\text{Area of face} = 9 \times 4$$
$$= 36 \text{ cm}^2$$

3. Calculate the area of one of the side faces.

$$\text{Area of face} = 4 \times 5$$
$$= 20 \text{ cm}^2$$

4. The surface area is calculated by taking 2 lots of these areas and adding them together.

$$\text{Surface area} = (2 \times 45) + (2 \times 36) + (2 \times 20)$$
$$= 90 + 72 + 40$$
$$= 202 \text{ cm}^2$$

To work out the surface area of harder 3D shapes, you can draw a net to help.

Example 3

What is the surface area of this triangular prism?

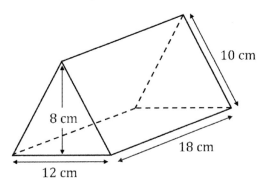

1. Draw a net of the prism.

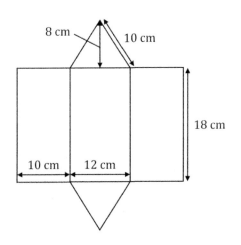

2. Work out the area of the left or right rectangle face (there are 2 with the same area).

Area of face $= 10 \times 18$
$= 180$ cm^2

3. Work out the area of the middle rectangle face.

Area of face $= 12 \times 18$
$= 216$ cm^2

4. Calculate the area of one of the triangle faces (there are 2 with the same area).

Area of face $= 12 \times 8 \div 2$
$= 48$ cm^2

5. Calculate the surface area by adding up the areas of all of the faces.

Surface area $= 180 + 180 + 216 + 48 + 48$
$= 672$ cm^2

Example 4

The net of a cylinder is shown below.

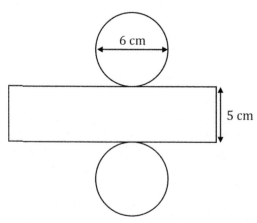

What is the surface area of the cylinder?
Use $\pi = 3.14$

1. Work out the circumference of the cylinder.

$$\text{Circumference} = \pi \times d$$
$$= 3.14 \times 6$$
$$= 18.84 \text{ cm}$$

2. Calculate the area of the rectangle (the curved face).

$$\text{Area of face} = 5 \times 18.84$$
$$= 94.2 \text{ cm}^2$$

3. Calculate the area of one of the circular faces (there are 2 with the same area).

$$r = d \div 2 = 6 \div 2 = 3 \text{ cm}$$

$$\text{Area of face} = \pi \times r^2$$
$$= 3.14 \times 3^2$$
$$= 3.14 \times 3 \times 3$$
$$= 28.26 \text{ cm}^2$$

4. Calculate the surface area, by adding up the areas of the faces.

$$\text{Surface area} = 94.2 + 28.26 + 28.26$$
$$= 150.72 \text{ cm}^2$$

For more revision, example questions and worksheets, scan this QR code:

2.16 Plans and Elevations

Projections are the different ways you can represent a 3D shape in 2D:

- A front elevation is a view looking at the shape from the front.
- A side elevation is a view looking at the shape from the side.
- A plan is a bird's eye view (looking at the shape from directly above).

Example 1

Draw a front elevation, a side elevation, and a plan for this 3D shape.

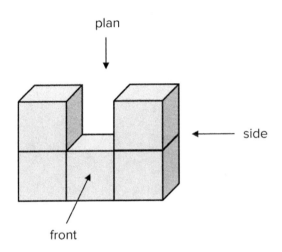

1. Standing at the front looking at the shape, you would see a u-shape, with 3 squares wide and 1 square on top at either side.

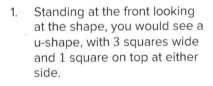

2. Standing at the side looking at the shape, you would see a width of 1 square and a height of 2 squares.

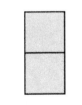

3. Looking at the shape from above, you would see a width of 3 squares and a length of 1 square.

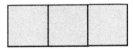

For more complex 3D shapes, you may be given the dimensions of the shape that you will need to use to draw the plans and elevations.

Example 2

An architect is planning a 3D structure seen below.

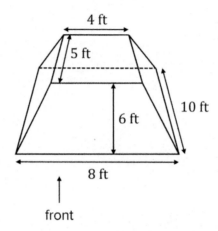

Draw the front elevation of this structure on the square grid below.

1 square = 1 ft in real life.

1. The width of the bottom of the front elevation is 8 ft, so this is 8 squares wide on the grid.

2. The width of the top of the front elevation is 4 ft, so this is 4 squares wide on the grid.

3. The middle of these two lines need to be inline, and need to be 6 squares apart vertically.

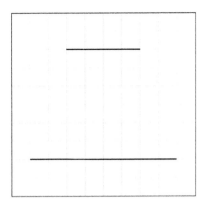

4. Join up the two lines to make the front elevation.

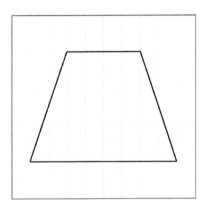

For more revision, example questions and worksheets, scan this QR code:

2.17 Maps and Scale Drawings

Scale drawings are used to represent larger or smaller objects, drawings, images or maps. A scale factor is used to accurately scale up or down a drawing. Scale drawings will come with a key, or scale factor, that will tell you what the dimension in the drawing is equal to in real life. They are usually represented as ratios, with an = sign or as a line drawing.

The 1 cm grid below show how some of these may look:

1 cm = 100 m	- 1 cm on the grid represents 100 m
1 : 10000	- 1 cm on the graph means 10000 cm in real life
100 m	- the distance marked represents 100 m

Notice that these all mean the same thing in this case.

You may be given a scale drawing with a grid background, like above, that will make questions easy. If you are not given a grid background, then you will need to use a ruler to measure line drawings and distances.

For the following examples you may get different lengths using a ruler – these examples are just for demonstration.

Example 1

The scale drawing below shows a section of coastline. Calculate the distance between point A and point B.

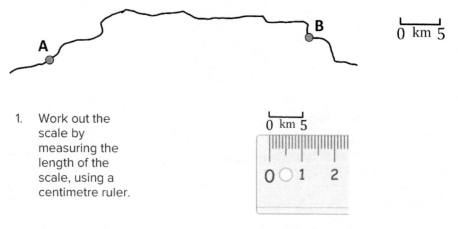

1. Work out the scale by measuring the length of the scale, using a centimetre ruler.

So, the scale means 1 cm on the drawing represents 5 km in real life.

2. Measure the distance between A and B, using the ruler.

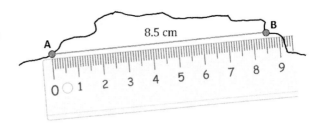

3. Find the real-life distance, by multiplying the scale by the distance measured on the drawing.

$$5 \times 8.5 = 42.5 \text{ km}$$

Example 2

Below is a map of Africa. Calculate the real-life distance between Dakar and Khartoum, marked on the map.

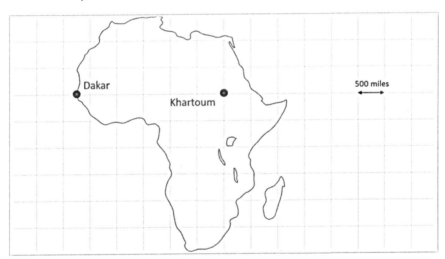

1. Work out the scale. The scale is given as a line drawing on the grid.

1 square = 500 miles

2. Count the number of squares between Dakar and Khartoum on the map.

5.5 squares

3. Find the real-life distance by multiplying the number of squares by the distance represented by one square (the scale).

$$5.5 \times 500 = 2750 \text{ miles}$$

You could be asked to find the scale on a map or drawing, given a distance, or you may be asked to make a scale drawing.

Example 3

The diagram below is a scale drawing of a racing car. The length of the car in real life is 4.4 m. Calculate the scale used in the drawing. Give your answer as a ratio.

1. Measure the length of the drawing, using a ruler centimetre.

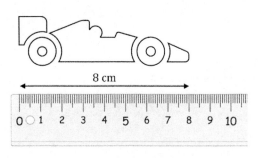

2. Convert the real-life length of the car to cm.

$$4.4 \text{ m} = 440 \text{ cm}$$

3. Write the ratio of the length in the drawing to the length in real life.

$$8 : 440$$

4. Simplify the ratio, by dividing both sides by 8.

$$1 : 55$$

This means that 1 cm on the drawing represents 55 cm in real life.

Example 4

Draw a rectangle, on the grid below, of height 2.5 m and width 3 m.

Use the scale 1:50. Each square is 1 cm by 1 cm.

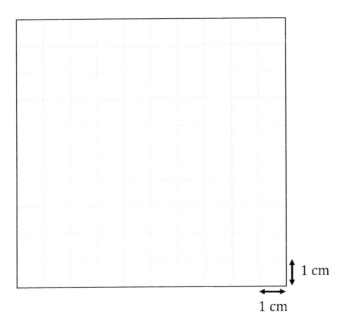

1 cm

1 cm

1. The grid is in cm, so convert the dimensions of the rectangle to cm.

   Real height = 2.5 × 100 = 250 cm
   Real width = 3 × 100 = 300 cm

2. 1:50 means 1 cm on the grid represents 50 cm in real life. So, divide the real dimensions by 50 to find the dimensions in the scale drawing.

   Drawing height = 250 ÷ 50 = 5 cm
   Drawing width = 300 ÷ 50 = 6 cm

3. Draw the rectangle on the grid, of height 5 cm and width 6 cm.

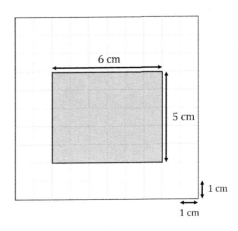

6 cm

5 cm

1 cm

1 cm

For more revision, example questions and worksheets, scan this QR code:

2.18 Coordinates

Coordinates are used to describe the positions of points on a grid in terms of their positions along the x-axis (horizontal) and y-axis (vertical).

Points can be plotted, and lines can be drawn on grids similar to that seen below.

- A grid is made by 2 lines crossing called axes, meeting at a point in the middle called the origin.
- The x-axis is the horizontal axis (left to right) and the y-axis is the vertical axis (bottom to top).
- Coordinates are described by a pair of numbers (x, y) and are represented by a dot or a cross. The x coordinate is always written first and the y coordinate is always written second.
- The origin has coordinates $(0, 0)$.

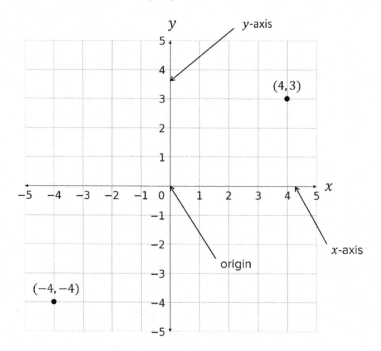

You may be asked to either find the coordinates of a point on the grid, or plot a point on a grid if you are given its coordinates.

Example 1

What are the coordinates of the point A on the grid below?

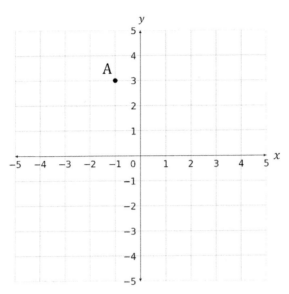

1. For the x coordinate, go down from A to the horizontal axis. Read off the number.

2. For the y coordinate, go across from A to the vertical axis. Read off the number.

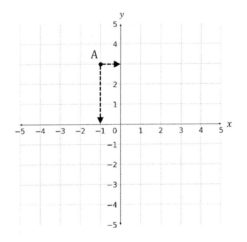

3. Put the two numbers in brackets with a comma separating them, with the x coordinate first.

$(-1, 3)$

Example 2

Plot the point $(2, 4)$ on the grid below.

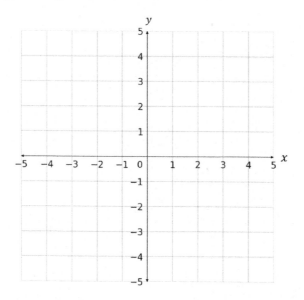

1. Move right from the origin until you find 2 on the horizontal axis.

2. Move up from 2 until you are level with 4 on the vertical axis.

3. Mark this position with a dot or cross, and label it $(2, 4)$.

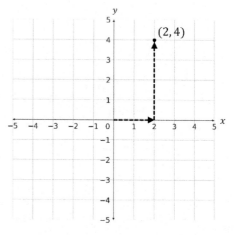

You can connect points on a grid to make lines or 2D shapes. You could be given dimensions in a question and have to use these to plot points and create 2D shapes.

Example 3

For the grid below, find the coordinates of C and D such that the rectangle ABCD has an area of 15 cm². On the grid 1 square = 1 cm.

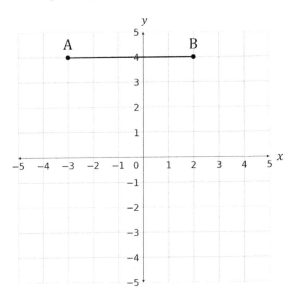

1. Find the distance between A and B.

   5 squares = 5 cm

2. The area of the rectangle is 15 cm², so divide the area by the length of AB to find the length of the shorter side.

   15 ÷ 5 = 3 cm

3. ABCD is a rectangle, points C and D must be directly below A and B. So, their y-coordinates will be 3 less than A and B.

   C is (2, 1)
   D is (−3, 1)

For more revision, example questions and worksheets, scan this QR code:

2.19 Angles in 2D Shapes

You will need to know how to find missing angles in triangles and quadrilaterals, using certain properties of these 2D shapes.

If you add up each angle in a triangle, the answer will always be 180°:

$$A + B + C = 180°$$

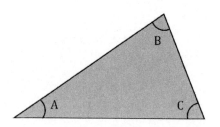

You can then use this rule to find the missing angles in triangles, together with some properties of triangles such as all angles in an equilateral triangle being equal, or two angles in an isosceles triangle being equal.

Example 1

Find the missing angle labelled A in this triangle.

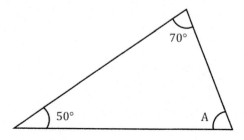

All three angles add up to 180°. So, find the missing angle by subtracting the two known angles from 180°.

$$A = 180° - 70° - 50°$$
$$= 60°$$

Example 2

Find the missing angles in this isosceles triangle below.

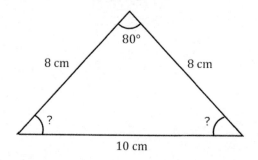

1. Subtract 80° from 180° to find the total of the missing angles.

$$180° - 80° = 100°$$

2. An isosceles triangle has two equal angles, so divide the total of the missing angles by 2 to find the value of both missing angles.

$$100° \div 2 = 50°$$

If you add up each angle in a quadrilateral, the answer will always be 360°:

$$A + B + C + D = 360°$$

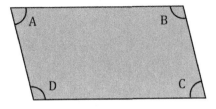

You can then use this rule to find missing angles in quadrilaterals, together with some properties of quadrilaterals such as lines of symmetry and equal angles.

Example 3

Find the missing angle labelled A in the quadrilateral below.

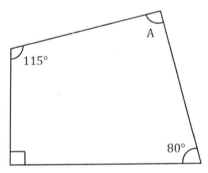

All four angles add up to 360°. So, find the missing angle by subtracting the three known angles (including the right angle which is 90°) from 360°.

$$A = 360° - 115° - 90° - 80°$$
$$= 75°$$

Example 4

The diagram to the below shows a quadrilateral with two lines of symmetry. Find the values of angles A, B and C.

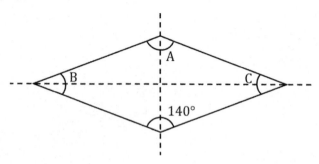

1. There are two lines of symmetry, meaning there are two pairs of equal angles.

    $A = 140°$
    $B = C$

2. Find the sum of angles B and C, by subtracting the two known angles from 360°.

    $360° - 140° - 140° = 80°$

3. Divide the total of the missing angles by 2 to find the value of B and C.

    $80 \div 2 = 40°$

    $B = 40°$ and $C = 40°$

For more revision, example questions and worksheets, scan this QR code:

Practice Questions – Measures, Shape and Space

Q1) Dylan weighs himself and he is 76 kg. What does he weigh in pounds (lb)?
Use the conversion rate 1 kg = 2.2 lb.
[1 mark]

Q2) Use the conversion graph below to determine whether 5.2 miles or 8 kilometres is greater.

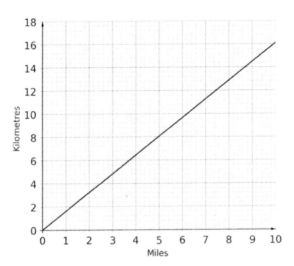

[2 marks]

Q3) Sean buys an antique chair. He buys the chair for £85 and spends £35 on restoring it. He then sells the chair for £150. Calculate the percentage profit in selling the chair.
[3 marks]

Q4) A supermarket sells two packs of toilet roll. Type A is a 6-pack costing £1.62. Type B is a 20-pack costing £6.50. Type B then has an offer of 20% off its original price. Which pack of toilet rolls is the better value for money?
[3 marks]

Q5) Lenny is saving up to buy a games console. He puts £400 in a savings account that pays 2% compound interest per annum. After 3 years, he takes his money out to pay for the games console. The games console costs £425. Does Lenny have enough money to pay for the games console?
[3 marks]

Q6) Milo visits a restaurant with his family. They spend £120.50 on food and £36.20 on drinks. The food they consume has 20% VAT (value-added tax) added on. Milo pays the bill. How much will this cost Milo?
[2 marks]

Q7) A motorcycle travels at 20 km/h for 42 minutes. Calculate the distance the motorcycle travels.
[2 marks]

Q8) An object has a mass of 300 g and a volume of 620 cm^3. Calculate the density of this object in g/cm^3. Give your answer to 3 decimal places.
[2 marks]

Q9) Derek has a post-it note in the shape of a square, seen in the diagram below.

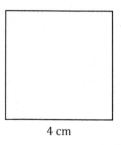

4 cm

Find the perimeter of the post-it note.
[2 marks]

Q10) Find the area of the triangle below.

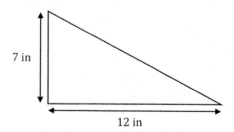

7 in

12 in

[2 marks]

Q11) A circle has a diameter of 5.4 mm. Calculate the area of the circle. Use $\pi = 3.14$.
[2 marks]

Q12) What is the name of this 3D shape?

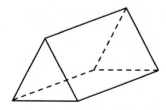

[1 mark]

Q13) Calculate the volume of this cylinder.

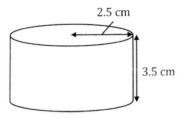

2.5 cm

3.5 cm

Use $\pi = 3.14$
Give your answer to 2 decimal places.
[3 marks]

Q14) Mary has an empty sandpit that she wants to fill. The sandpit is in the shape of a cuboid. Its dimensions are 1.2 m × 0.6 m × 0.4 m. An individual bag of sand has a volume of 0.04 m³. Each bag of sand costs £22.50. Calculate how much it would cost for Mary to fill the sandpit.
[4 marks]

Q15) The net of a shape is drawn below. Which 3D shape does this net belong to?

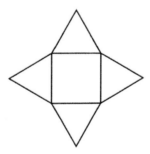

[1 mark]

Q16) Calculate the surface area of the cuboid seen in the diagram below.

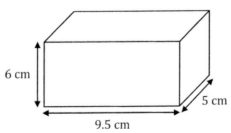

6 cm

5 cm

9.5 cm

[3 marks]

Q17) Draw a front elevation and side elevation of this shape.

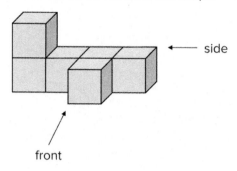

side

front

[2 marks]

Q18) The diagram below shows a scale drawing of Darwin's bedroom. Given that 1 cm on the diagram represents 0.6 m in real life, find the actual width of Darwin's bedroom.

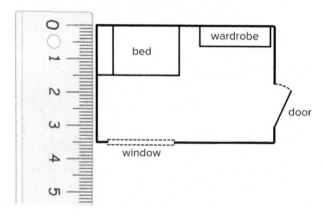

[2 marks]

Q19) Which letter on the grid represents the point with coordinates $(-2, -1)$?

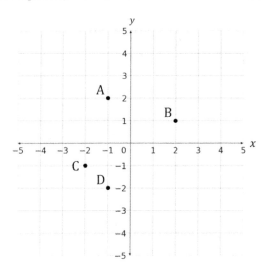

[1 mark]

Q20) A parallelogram has two pairs of equal angles. Find the missing angles labelled A and B in the diagram below.

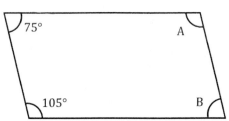

[2 marks]

3 Handling Information and Data

3.1 Mean, Median, Mode and Range

The mean, median and the mode are different measures of the average value of a set of data. The range is a measure of spread.

When you hear someone talking about an average they will usually be referring to the mean. To calculate the mean you add up all of the values in the set of data and divide by the amount of values in the set of data:

$$\text{Mean} = \frac{\text{Total of values}}{\text{Number of values}}$$

Example 1

Harriet measures the weights of her 5 hamsters and writes them in a list:

$$120 \text{ g}, 105 \text{ g}, 98 \text{ g}, 125 \text{ g}, 114 \text{ g}$$

What is the mean weight of the hamsters?

1. Add up the numbers to work out the total of values.

$$120 + 105 + 98 + 125 + 114 = 562 \text{ g}$$

2. Count the number of values in the list.

$$5$$

3. Divide the total of values by the number of values to find the mean.

$$\text{Mean} = \frac{562}{5} = 112.4 \text{ g}$$

The median is the 'middle number' of a data set where the numbers are in order of size. To calculate the median, use the following method:

1. Cross out the first and last numbers, then the second and second last numbers and so on, working inwards.
2. Eventually you will be left with one or two numbers.
3. If only one number is left, this is the median. If two numbers are left, the median is halfway between the two numbers – add the two numbers together and divide by 2 to find halfway.

Example 2

Hillary records the amount of money she spent on food in the last 8 weeks:

$$£38, £32, £40, £21, £28, £38, £50, £26$$

Work out the median amount of money Hillary spends.

1. Put the list in order from smallest to largest.

   £21, £26, £28, £32, £38, £38, £40, £50

2. Cross out the first and last numbers, then the second and second last numbers, and so on, working inwards

   ~~£21~~, ~~£26~~, ~~£28~~, £32, £38, ~~£38~~, ~~£40~~, ~~£50~~

3. There are 8 data values, so the median is halfway between the 4th and 5th values. Add up the 4th and 5th values and divide by 2 to find the median.

   $$\text{Median} = \frac{£32 + £38}{2}$$
   $$= £35$$

The mode of a set of data is the most common value that appears. You can arrange the values in order of size to make the mode easier to work out, however this is not necessary.

Example 3

Find the mode of this set of data:

$$7, 10, 4, 3, 4, 8, 2, 5, 4, 2$$

1. Arrange the numbers in order from smallest to largest.

   $$2, 2, 3, 4, 4, 4, 5, 7, 8, 10$$

2. Find the number that appears the most. This is the mode.

   Mode = 4
   (this appears the most – 3 times)

The range is the difference between the largest and smallest values in a set of data.

$$\text{Range} = \text{largest value} - \text{smallest value}$$

Again, you can write the values in order from smallest to largest first but it is not essential.

Example 4

Susie records the height of her 6 friends:

$$160 \text{ cm}, 172 \text{ cm}, 164 \text{ cm}, 148 \text{ cm}, 175 \text{ cm}, 170 \text{ cm}$$

Calculate the range in the in heights.

1. Spot the smallest value and the largest value.

   Smallest value = 148 cm
   Largest value = 175 cm

2. Subtract the smallest value from the largest value to find the range.

   Range = 175 − 148
   = 27 cm

Averages can be used to make estimates and predict values. For example, if you know a weekly average, then you can assume that every week in a year has this average value. Therefore, you can multiply this average by 52 (the number of weeks in a year) to predict the value for a whole year.

Example 5

Mick spends £260 on his credit card in May, £330 on his credit card in June and £310 on his credit card in July. Calculate the mean to estimate how much Mick will spend on his credit card in one year.

1. Calculate the mean and assume he will spend this amount each month.

   $$\text{Mean} = \frac{£260 + £330 + £310}{3}$$
   $$= £300$$

2. Multiply this by 12 to estimate the amount he will spend on his credit card in one year.

   $£12 \times 300 = £3600$

For more revision, example questions and worksheets, scan this QR code:

3.2 Comparing Data Sets

You can use averages and ranges to compare different data sets in real world contexts.

For the average, you tend to use the mean. You could use the median or the mode, but they do not consider all of the data. There also may not be a mode if there are no repeated values.

Example 1

The table below shows the sales from car dealership from two weeks.

Week	Number of Cars Sold						
	Mon	Tue	Wed	Thu	Fri	Sat	Sun
1	12	15	16	13	13	15	-
2	15	16	10	14	16	25	-

Which week has the better average sales figures?

1. Work out the mean for week 1.

$$\text{Mean} = \frac{12 + 15 + 16 + 13 + 13 + 15}{6}$$

$$= 14$$

2. Work out the mean for week 2.

$$\text{Mean} = \frac{15 + 16 + 10 + 14 + 16 + 25}{6}$$

$$= 16$$

3. Compare the means.

The mean is higher for week 2, so week 2 has better average sales figures.

The range is used to show how consistent or varied sets of data are. A small range means the data is consistent and a large range means the data is varied and not consistent.

Example 2

The table below shows the same sales from the car dealership from two weeks.

Week	Number of Cars Sold						
	Mon	Tue	Wed	Thu	Fri	Sat	Sun
1	12	15	16	13	13	15	-
2	15	16	10	14	16	25	-

Which week has the most consistent sales figures?

1. Work out the range for week 1.

Range = 16 − 12
= 4

2. Work out the range for week 2.

Range = 25 − 10
= 15

3. Compare the ranges.

Week 1 has the smallest range, so week 1 has the most consistent sales figures.

For more revision, example questions and worksheets, scan this QR code:

3.3 Estimating the Mean

You will often be presented with grouped data in the form of a grouped frequency table. Grouped frequency tables are a useful way of displaying data by grouping data into classes. For example, the frequency table below shows the number of points a group of students had after playing a game.

Number of Points	Frequency
0 − 15	4
16 − 30	5
31 − 40	1
41 − 50	6
51 − 60	6

There are some things to be aware of when dealing with these:

- Classes don't overlap, i.e. if the second class was instead 15 − 30, then someone who had 15 points would fit into the first two classes. This wouldn't work.
- In this example, all of the data is known. However, if you didn't know the greatest number, then the last class could be "51 or more" for example.
- The frequency column tells you how many for each class, e.g. 4 people had between 0 and 15 points.

You can use data from grouped frequency tables to estimate the mean of the data. The reason you will be 'estimating' is because you will not know how the data is distributed in each class – it could all be at the lower end of the class, all at the higher end or evenly distributed throughout.

To estimate the mean from a grouped frequency table, use these following steps:

1. Add a 'midpoint' column and a 'frequency × midpoint' column to the table.
2. Find the midpoint of each class and write these in the 'midpoint' column. The midpoint is exactly halfway between the class.
3. Work out the 'frequency × midpoint' for each row by multiplying the numbers in the 'frequency' column by the numbers in the 'midpoint column'. Write these in the final column.
4. Calculate the total 'frequency' by adding up the numbers in the 'frequency' column and calculate the total 'frequency × midpoint' by adding up the numbers in the 'frequency × midpoint' column.
5. Estimate the mean, using

Estimated mean $=$ (Total 'frequency $\times$ midpoint') $\div$ (Total 'frequency')

Example 1

The frequency table below shows the number of days of holiday a group of workers have left to take in the remaining year.

Days of Holiday	Frequency
0 – 4	10
5 – 9	8
10 – 14	12
15 – 19	8
20 – 24	2

Estimate the mean number of days of holiday left to work.

1. Add a 'midpoint' column and a 'frequency × midpoint' column.

2. Calculate the midpoint for each row and add them to the 'midpoint' column, e.g. the midpoint of 0 and 4 is 2.

Days of Holiday	Frequency	Midpoint	Frequency × midpoint
0 – 4	10	2	
5 – 9	8	7	
10 – 14	12	12	
15 – 19	8	17	
20 – 24	2	22	

3. Work out the 'frequency × midpoint' for each row and add them to the 'frequency × midpoint' column, e.g. for the first row, 10 × 2 = 20.

4. Work out the totals for the 'frequency' column and the 'frequency × midpoint' column, by adding up the numbers.

Days of Holiday	Frequency	Midpoint	Frequency × midpoint
0 – 4	10	2	20
5 – 9	8	7	56
10 – 14	12	12	144
15 – 19	8	17	136
20 – 24	2	22	44
Total	40		400

5. Estimate the mean.

Estimated mean = 400 ÷ 40
= 10

For more revision, example questions and worksheets, scan this QR code:

3.4 Probability

Probability is a measurement of the likelihood of an event happening. You may see fractions, decimals and percentages being used to describe probabilities.

The probability scale summarises the likelihood of an event occurring:

- At the lower end of the scale, the likelihood of an event occurring is very small, so the probability is close to 0 (or 0%).
- As you move up the scale, events become increasingly likely.
- When the probability is 0.5 (or $\frac{1}{2}$ or 50%), there is an equal chance of an event occurring/not occurring.
- If the probability is less than 0.5, the event is unlikely to occur.
- If the probability is greater than 0.5, the event is likely to occur.
- Events that are impossible have a probability of 0 and events that are certain have a probability of 1 (or 100%).

This information is summarised in the figure below:

You may sometimes see notation like P(event) which means the probability of an event happening. The word in the brackets is interchangeable with what the event is, e.g. you may see P(even) which means the probability of something being even, or P(blue) which means the probability of something being blue.

To find the probability of an event happening, you divide the number of ways that an event can happen by the total number of possible outcomes:

$$\text{Probability} = \frac{\text{number of outcomes in event}}{\text{total number of possible outcomes}}$$

Example 1

Maurice has 3 white shirts and 7 black shirts in his wardrobe. He picks out a shirt at random. What is the probability that he picks a white shirt? Write your answer as a decimal.

a) Calculate the total number of shirts in his wardrobe.

$$3 + 7 = 10$$

b) Calculate the probability of him picking a white shirt, by dividing the number of ways of picking a white shirt by the total number of ways of picking a shirt.

$$\text{Probability} = \frac{3}{10}$$
$$= 0.3$$

All probabilities must add up to 1 (or 100%), so to find the probability of an event not happening by subtracting the probability that it will happen from 1:

$$\text{Probability of event not happening} = 1 - \text{probability of event happening}$$

Example 2

The probability of Venus winning a game of tennis is 0.7. What is the probability of her not winning the game?

Subtract the probability of her winning from 1.

Probability that Venus does not win
$$= 1 - \text{probability that Venus does win}$$
$$= 1 - 0.7$$
$$= 0.3$$

You can find the probability of an event happening multiple times by multiplying the probability of it happening once by itself that number of times.

Example 3

The probability of rolling an even number on a fair six-sided die is 0.5. It is rolled three times. What is the probability of landing on an even number on all three occasions?

Multiply together three lots of 0.5 since the die is rolled three times.

$$\text{Probability} = 0.5 \times 0.5 \times 0.5$$
$$= 0.125$$

For more revision, example questions and worksheets, scan this QR code:

3.5 Probability Tables

You may need to use tables or diagrams to help you find probabilities. One type of table you will encounter is a two-way table.

Example 1

The table below shows some information about which class students in a year group are in.

	Class X	Class Y	Total
Boys	22		39
Girls	20		
Total		38	80

a)   Complete the two-way table.

1.   Find the missing values in the table by adding or subtracting within rows or columns.

Class X total $= 22 + 20 = 42$
Class Y Boys $= 39 - 22 = 17$
Class Y Girls $= 38 - 17 = 21$
Girls total $= 80 - 39 = 41$

2.   Fill in the missing gaps with these values.

	Class X	Class Y	Total
Boys	22	17	39
Girls	20	21	41
Total	42	38	80

This could have been done in a different order with different sums.

b)   A student from Class Y is chosen at random. What is the probability that they are a boy?

1.   Find the number of boys in Class Y and find the Class Y total.

Boys in Class Y $= 17$
Class Y total $= 38$

2.   The probability is written as the number of boys in class Y divided by the Class Y total.

$$\text{Probability} = \frac{17}{38}$$

When there are two events happening, it is helpful to write down all possible results in a table for multiple events. You can then find probabilities using the table.

Example 2

Two 4 sided spinners are spun and their outcomes are multiplied together. The first spinner is numbered 1, 2, 3, 4 and the second spinner is numbered 1, 3, 5, 7. What is the probability that the result is less than 10?

1. Draw a table, with the first spinner on the top and the second spinner down the side, with the numbers on the spinners along the top and the side also.

Spinner Two	×	1	2	3	4
	1				
	3				
	5				
	7				

(Spinner One along top)

2. Fill in the table, by multiplying the numbers in each row by the numbers in each column, i.e. if you land on 2 on the first spinner and 5 on the second spinner, then you multiply the numbers together to get $2 \times 5 = 10$.

Spinner Two	×	1	2	3	4
	1	1	2	3	4
	3	3	6	9	12
	5	5	10	15	20
	7	7	14	21	28

(Spinner One along top)

3. Find how many results are less than 10 (you could circle them to make it clearer), and how many results there are in total.

Results less that 10 = 9
Results in total = 16

4. The probability is written as the number of results less than 10 divided by the total number of results.

$$\text{Probability} = \frac{9}{16}$$

For more revision, example questions and worksheets, scan this QR code:

3.6 Scatter Graphs

Scatter graphs are used to determine the existence and type of correlation between two variables. If the graph shows a relationship between the variables, we say they have correlation. There are two types of correlation:

- Positive correlation – as one variable goes up, the other also goes up.
- Negative correlation – as one variable goes up, the other goes down.

If the points are randomly spread, we say there is no correlation.

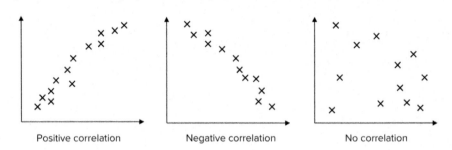

Positive correlation   Negative correlation   No correlation

You need to be able to draw scatter graphs accurately.

Example 1

The table below shows the results of some students' Maths and English exams out of 100. Plot a scatter graph for this data.

Maths Mark	38	62	18	75	38	59	66	92	52	75	48
English Mark	74	44	85	19	88	69	50	33	29	32	56

1. Draw the axes. One should be for the 'Maths mark', making sure it goes up to at least 100 and the other should be for the 'English Mark', making sure it goes up to at least 100 also. Label the axes.

2. Plot the data (similar to plotting coordinates) e.g. for someone who got 38 on their maths exam and 74 on their English exam, go across to 38 on the x-axis and then up to 74 on the y-axis, and draw a cross or a dot.

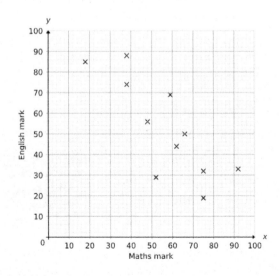

A line of best fit is a straight line that is used to represent the correlation of the data. Lines of best fit should go through the middle of all the points, with an equal number of points on either side of the line.

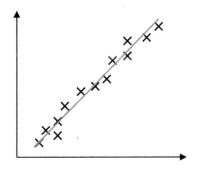

If you know one value on a scatter graph, you can use a line of best fit to predict the other value.

Example 2

Predict the English mark of someone that scored a mark of 60 in Maths, using the same scatter graph from before.

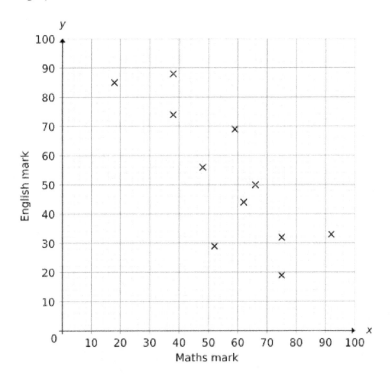

1. Draw a line of best fit through the points, with roughly an equal number of points on either side of the line.

2. To find the English mark of someone who scored 60 in maths, go up from 60 on the horizontal axis until you meet the line.

3. Go across until you meet the vertical axis.

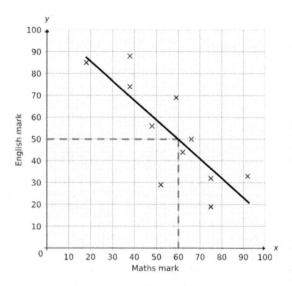

4. Read off the value.

Predicted English mark = 50

For more revision, example questions and worksheets, scan this QR code:

Practice Questions – Handling Information and Data

Q1) Find the mode of these numbers:

$$4, 5, 2, 4, 2, 3, 5, 4, 4, 1, 7, 2$$

[1 mark]

Q2) An ice cream stall records the amount of money they make over the last 8 days.

$$£242, £250, £278, £203, £298, £346, £210, £200$$

Calculate the median amount of money made.
[2 marks]

Q3) The table below shows the download speed of two broadband providers in a particular area for 5 consecutive days.

Day	Broadband Speed (Mb per second)				
	Mon	Tue	Wed	Thu	Fri
RapidB	42.7	41.6	40.1	43.9	34.1
FastWeb1000	53.2	53.9	50.7	57.4	55.3

Which company has the most consistent download speed over the 5 days?
[2 marks]

Q4) Heidi has 4 days off in June, 2 days off in July and 6 days off in August. Calculate the mean and use this to estimate how many days she will have off in one whole year.
[2 marks]

Q5) The table below shows some information about the number of sweatshirts a shop sells each week over the last 12 weeks.

Number of sweatshirts	Frequency
0 – 12	3
13 – 25	1
26 – 36	3
37 – 43	2
44 – 50	3

Work out an estimate for the average number of sweatshirts sold each week.
[4 marks]

Q6) There are 300 raffle tickets in a hat. 15 of the tickets correspond to winning prizes. Roberto picks out a raffle ticket out of the hat at random. What is the probability that he wins a prize? Give your answer as a decimal.
[2 marks]

Q7) Lionel has a 92% chance of being fit to play a football match. What is the probability that he won't be fit?

[1 mark]

Q8) The table below shows some information about the number of home and away fans at a football match.

	Adult	Child	Total
Home		37	149
Away	40		
Total		48	200

By completing the table, find the probability that an adult chosen at random is an away fan.

[3 marks]

Q9) What type of correlation, if any, does this scatter graph show?

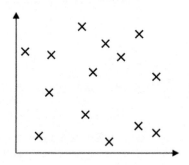

[1 mark]

Q10) Draw a line of best fit on the scatter graph below.

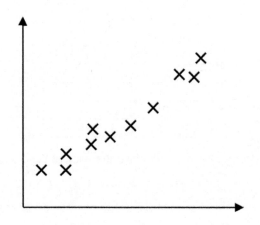

[1 mark]

110

Exam Tips

Here are some exam tips to help you pass your exam.

Read the Exam Instructions

It will tell you useful things, including how much time your exam lasts, how long you should spend on each section, whether or not you can use a calculator, that you should show your working, what stationery you need, and much more!

Show Your Working

Even if you get the answer wrong, if you show your working you could still get marks for a question – indeed in a lot of questions only one mark is awarded for seeing the correct answer, and the rest are for correct working.

Show You Have Checked

When a question asks for you to show you have checked your answer, you should NOT just say "used a calculator". Instead, you should do a key calculation from your working backwards. If you multiplied by 7 to get the final answer, divide the final answer by 7. If you added 34 to get the final answer, subtract 34 from the final answer. Make sure you get back to the number you expect to see.

Checking Your Answer

Even if the question does not ask you to check your answer, you should still check your answer to make sure it is correct. Once you have finished a question, do a key calculation from your working backwards to check it is correct. If you have time at the end of the exam, go back through it and check all of your answers.

Units

You should ALWAYS add units to your answer where appropriate. Many questions contain a mark for correct units.

Memorise until you can't take it anymore

You should try to memorise everything in the formula booklet – and in any case have most of it memorised before you take your exam. If you are struggling to memorise something important but cannot delay your exam, spend some time in the minutes leading up to your exam trying to memorise it, then the moment your exam starts write it on the inside front cover of your paper.

Distribution of Marks

Here is an example of how marks would be distributed for the answers to a typical exam question:

Ellie buys 5 books for £12.50 at a second-hand book shop.
She sold three of them for £9.00 and the other two for £6.00.
Ellie thinks she has made a profit of 20% of the cost of the books.
Is Ellie correct?
Show your working.

[4 marks]

Where are the 4 marks in this question?

The first mark is for finding the total money Ellie made in selling the books.

$$£9.00 + £6.00 = £15.00$$

The second mark is for finding how much profit she has made.

$$£15.00 - £12.50 = £2.50$$

The third mark is for finding 20% of the cost of the books.

$$20\% = \times 0.2$$

$$£12.50 \times 0.2 = £2.50$$

The final mark is for concluding based on your calculations.

$$\text{Ellie is correct.}$$

Don't worry if you get one of the calculations wrong and reach the wrong conclusion because of it. While you won't get the mark for that calculation, you might still get all the other marks, since your conclusion was right from your results.

Use Your Common Sense

You can use your common sense to check that your answer is reasonable.

For example, if your answer for a number of people is not a whole number, something has gone wrong. Or, if an answer is far too big or small, such as if you calculated the length of a driveway to be 100000 metres, something has gone wrong.

This can be your most powerful tool, as it helps you spot mistakes almost as soon as you make them, so you can correct them and move on quickly, ensuring success in your exam.

Functional Skills Maths Level 2 Course

You
are
unique...

 Virtual **exam mocks**

 **Personalised** topic recommendations

 Detailed **video explanations**

 **100's** of practice questions

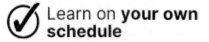 Learn on **your own schedule**

 **Expertly designed** course

Shouldn't your
learning
be too?

Get learning at pfs.la/courses

Formulas

Here is a summary of some key formulas and rules you will need to remember for your exam.

Square Numbers

The square of a number, written as n^2, is itself multiplied by itself.

Example: $5^2 = 5 \times 5 = 25$

Percentages

15% of $= \times 0.15$

15% increase $= \times 1.15$

15% decrease/discount $= \times 0.85$
(because $100 - 15 = 85$)

Common Fractions, Decimals and Percentages

Fraction	Decimal	Percentage
$\dfrac{1}{2}$	0.5	50%
$\dfrac{1}{4}$	0.25	25%
$\dfrac{3}{4}$	0.75	75%
$\dfrac{1}{5}$	0.2	20%
$\dfrac{1}{10}$	0.1	10%
$\dfrac{1}{20}$	0.05	5%

Formulas

Some questions give you a formula to use.

Example: Time taken to wash car (mins) = 30 + 2 × surface area of car (m²)

Suppose we have a car with a surface area of 25 m². How long does it take to wash?

$$\text{Time} = 30 + 2 \times 25 = 80 \text{ mins}$$

Key Conversions

Length:
1 cm = 10 mm
1 m = 100 cm
1 km = 1000 m

Capacity:
1 L = 1000 ml
1 ml = 1 cm³
1000 L = 1 m³

Weight:
1 kg = 1000 g

Money:
£1 = 100p

Time:
1 minute = 60 seconds
1 hour = 60 minutes
1 day = 24 hours
1 week = 7 days
1 year = 365 days
1 year = 12 months
1 decade = 10 years
1 century = 100 years

Compound Interest

5% interest on £100 for 3 years:

$$\text{Total} = 100 \times 1.05 \times 1.05 \times 1.05 = £115.76$$

Speed, Distance and Time

$$\text{speed} = \text{distance} \div \text{time}$$

$$\text{distance} = \text{speed} \times \text{time}$$

$$\text{time} = \text{distance} \div \text{speed}$$

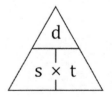

Density, Mass and Volume

$$\text{density} = \text{mass} \div \text{volume}$$

$$\text{mass} = \text{density} \times \text{volume}$$

$$\text{volume} = \text{mass} \div \text{density}$$

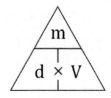

Perimeter

Square $= 4a$

Rectangle $= 2(a + b)$

Equilateral triangle $= 3a$

Isosceles triangle $= 2a + b$

Scalene triangle $= a + b + c$

n-sided regular polygon $= na$

Circle $= \pi d = 2\pi r$

Area

Square $= a^2$

Rectangle $= ab$

Triangle $= \frac{1}{2}bh$

Circle $= \pi r^2$

Volume

Cube $= a^3$

Cuboid $= abc$

Prism $=$ length $\times$ cross-sectional area

Cylinder $= \pi r^2 h$

Angles

Sum of angles in triangle $= 180°$

Sum of angles in quadrilateral $= 360°$

Mean and Range

$$\text{Mean} = \frac{\text{Total of values}}{\text{Number of values}}$$

Range $=$ largest value $-$ smallest value

Estimating the Mean

Estimated mean $=$ (Total 'frequency $\times$ midpoint') $\div$ (Total 'frequency')

Probability

$$\text{Probability} = \frac{\text{number of outcomes in event}}{\text{total number of possible outcomes}}$$

Probability of event not happening $= 1 -$ probability of event happening

Probability of event happening n times $=$ (Probability of event)^n

Practice Question Answers

Numbers

Q1)	Sixty-eight thousand, three hundred and seventy-three.	[1]
Q2)	$-278, 38, 286, 291, 301$	[1]
Q3)	14063	[1]
Q4)	324	[1]
Q5)	$558 \div 12 = 46.5$	[1]
	You can't have 46.5 biscuits, so she will only be able to make 46 biscuits.	[1]
Q6)	$6^2 \div (5 \times 2 - 7) = 36 \div 3$	[1]
	12	[1]
Q7)	$\dfrac{40}{75}$	[1]
	$\dfrac{8}{15}$	[1]
Q8)	$38520 \div 12 \times 5$	[1]
	16050 people voted for the red party.	[1]
Q9)	$3\dfrac{3}{8} - 1\dfrac{1}{4} = 3 - 1 + \dfrac{3}{8} - \dfrac{1}{4}$	
	$3 - 1 = 2$ and $\dfrac{3}{8} - \dfrac{1}{4} = \dfrac{3}{8} - \dfrac{2}{8} = \dfrac{1}{8}$	[1]
	$3\dfrac{3}{8} - 1\dfrac{1}{4} = 2 + \dfrac{1}{8} = 2\dfrac{1}{8}$	[1]
Q10)	135.366	[1]
Q11)	£4.80 rounds to £5, £1.85 rounds to £2, £11.10 rounds to £11	[1]
	$£5 + £2 + £11 = £18$	[1]
Q12)	$38\% = 10\% + 10\% + 10\% + 5\% + 1\% + 1\% + 1\%$	
	$= 80 + 80 + 80 + 40 + 8 + 8 + 8$	[1]
	$38\% = 304$	[1]
Q13)	12% decrease means you multiply by 0.88	
	$£15.50 \times 0.88$	[1]
	£13.64	[1]
Q14)	16% increase means you divide by 1.16	
	$£145 \div 1.16$	[1]
	£125	[1]
Q15)	$\dfrac{3}{4} = 3 \div 4 = 0.75$	
	$78\% = 78 \div 100 = 0.78$	
	$\dfrac{4}{5} = 4 \div 5 = 0.8$	
	$0.8, 0.79, 0.78, 0.75$	[1]
	$\dfrac{4}{5}, 0.79, 78\%, \dfrac{3}{4}$	[1]

Q16)	$3 + 5 + 2 = 10$ parts	[1]
	1 part $= 2500 \div 10 = 250$ ml	
	1st cup: $250 \times 3 = 750$ ml	
	2nd cup: $250 \times 5 = 1250$ ml	
	3rd cup: $250 \times 2 = 500$ ml	[1]
Q17)	1 part $= 280 \div 4 = 70$ ml	[1]
	Total parts $= 1 + 4 = 5$	
	$5 \times 70 = 350$ ml	[1]
Q18)	$200 \div 16 = 12.5$ g of flour needed per bun	[1]
	$12.5 \times 12 = 150$ g	[1]
Q19)	$3 \times 45 = 135$ minutes for 1 person	[1]
	$135 \div 5 = 27$ minutes	[1]
Q20)	Sally: £25 + £5 $\times 7 = $ £60	[1]
	Jessica: £8 $\times 7 = $ £56	[1]
	Sally spends the most money	[1]

Measures, Shape and Space

Q1)	$76 \times 2.2 = 167.2$ lb	[1]
Q2)	5.2 miles $= 8.4$ km or 8 km $= 5$ miles	[1]
	5.2 miles is greater than 8 km	[1]
Q3)	Costs $=$ £85 + £35 $=$ £120	[1]
	Profit $=$ £150 − £120 $=$ £30	[1]
	Percentage profit $= \frac{30}{120} \times 100 = 25\%$	[1]
Q4)	Type B cost $=$ £6.50 $\times 0.8 = $ £5.20	[1]
	Type A cost per roll $=$ £1.62 $\div 6 = $ £0.27	
	Type B cost per roll $=$ £5.20 $\div 20 = $ £0.26	[1]
	Type B is the better value for money.	[1]
Q5)	£400 $\times 1.02 \times 1.02 \times 1.02$	[1]
	£424.48	[1]
	No, he does not have enough money	[1]
Q6)	Food: £120.50 $\times 1.20 = $ £144.60	[1]
	Total cost $=$ £144.60 + £36.20 $=$ £180.80	[1]
Q7)	42 mins $= \dfrac{42}{60} = 0.7$ hours	
	distance $= 20 \times 0.7$	[1]
	14 km/h	[1]
Q8)	density $= 300 \div 620$	[1]
	0.484 g/cm^3 (3 dp)	[1]
Q9)	Perimeter $= 4 + 4 + 4 + 4$	[1]
	16 cm	[1]

Q10)	$\text{Area} = \dfrac{1}{2} \times 12 \times 7$	[1]
	42 sq. in	[1]
Q11)	$\text{Radius} = 5.4 \div 2 = 2.7 \text{ mm}$	
	$\text{Area} = 3.14 \times 2.7 \times 2.7$	[1]
	22.8906 mm^2	[1]
Q12)	Triangular prism	[1]
Q13)	$\text{area of circle} = 3.14 \times 2.5^2 = 3.14 \times 2.5 \times 2.5 = 19.625 \text{ cm}^2$	[1]
	$\text{volume} = 19.625 \times 3.5$	[1]
	$68.69 \text{ cm}^3 \text{ (2 dp)}$	[1]
Q14)	$\text{volume} = 1.2 \times 0.6 \times 0.4$	[1]
	0.288 cm^3	[1]
	$\text{bags needed} = 0.288 \div 0.04 = 7.2$	[1]
	8 bags needed	
	$8 \times £22.50 = £180$	[1]
Q15)	Square-based pyramid	[1]
Q16)	$\text{Surface area} = 2 \times (6 \times 9.5) + 2 \times (6 \times 5) + 2 \times (5 \times 9.5)$	[1]
	269 cm^2	[1]
Q17)		[1]
		[1]
Q18)	$\text{width} = 3.5 \text{ cm}$	[1]
	$\text{real life width} = 3.5 \times 0.6 = 2.1 \text{ m}$	[1]
Q19)	C	[1]
Q20)	$A = 105°$	[1]
	$B = 75°$	[1]

Handling Information and Data

Q1)	4	[1]
Q2)	in order: £200, £203, £210, £242, £250, £278, £298, £346 $$\text{median} = \frac{£242 + £250}{2}$$ £246	[1] [1]
Q3)	RapidB range = $43.9 - 34.1 = 9.8$ FastWeb1000 range = $57.4 - 50.7 = 6.7$ FastWeb1000 had the more consistent download speeds over the 5 days.	[1] [1]
Q4)	$$\text{mean} = \frac{4+2+6}{3} = 4$$ estimate $= 4 \times 12 = 48$ days off	[1] [1]
Q5)	 | Number of sweatshirts	Frequency	Midpoint	Midpoint × frequency
---	---	---	---
$0-12$	3	6	18
$13-25$	1	19	19
$26-36$	3	31	93
$37-43$	2	40	80
$44-50$	3	47	141 | total 'midpoint × frequency' $= 18 + 19 + 93 + 80 + 141 = 351$ $$\text{mean} = \frac{351}{12} = 29.25$$	[2] [1] [1]
Q6)	$$\text{probability} = \frac{15}{300}$$ 0.05	[1] [1]
Q7)	8%	[1]
Q8)	 |	Adult	Child	Total
---	---	---	---
Home	112	37	149
Away	40	11	51
Total	152	48	200 | $$\text{probability} = \frac{40}{152}$$	[2] [1]
Q9)	No correlation	[1]
Q10)		[1]

Functional Skills Maths Level 2
Revision Fundamentals

Printed in Great Britain
by Amazon

20456162R00071